ACHIEVE LEVEL 4

SCIENCE

By **Gerald Page**

RISING STARS

PLEASE NOTE: THIS BOOK MAY NOT BE PHOTOCOPIED OR REPRODUCED AND WE APPRECIATE YOUR HELP IN PROTECTING OUR COPYRIGHT.

Rising Stars UK Ltd., 22 Grafton Street, London W1S 4EX

www.risingstars-uk.com

Every effort has been made to trace copyright holders and obtain their permission for the use of copyright material. The authors and publishers will gladly receive information enabling them to rectify any error or omission in subsequent editions.

All facts are correct at time of going to press.

First published 2003
This edition 2007

Editorial: Tanya Solomons
Design: Clive Sutherland
Cover design: Burville-Riley Design
Illustrations: Burville-Riley Design; Beehive Illustration (Theresa Tibbetts); Graham-Cameron Illustration (Tony Maher), Jim Eldridge and Oxford Designers and Illustrators
Cover image: Beehive Illustration (Theresa Tibbetts)

British Library Cataloguing in Publication Data
A CIP record for this book is available from the British Library.

ISBN 978-1-84680-120-4

Printed by Craft Print International Ltd, Singapore

Contents

How to use this book

1. **Introduction** – This section tells you what you need to do to achieve a Level 4. It picks out the key learning objective and explains it simply to you.

2. **Self-assessment** – Colour in the face that best describes your understanding of this concept.

3. **Question** – The question helps you to learn by doing. It is presented in a similar way to a SATs question and gives you a real example to work with.

4. **Flow chart** – This shows you the steps to use when completing questions like this. Some of the advice appears on every flow chart, such as 'read the question then read it again'. This is because this is the best way of getting good marks on the test.
    This icon indicates the section is a *teaching* section.

5. **Tip boxes and Key Facts** – These provide test hints and general tips on getting the best marks in the tests.

WHAT WE HAVE INCLUDED:

- Those topics at Level 3 that are trickiest to get right.
- ALL Level 4 content so you know that you are covering all the topics that could come up in the test.
- We have also put in a big selection of our favourite test techniques, tips for revision and some advice on what the tests are all about, as well as the answers so you can see how well you are getting on.

GOOD LUCK!

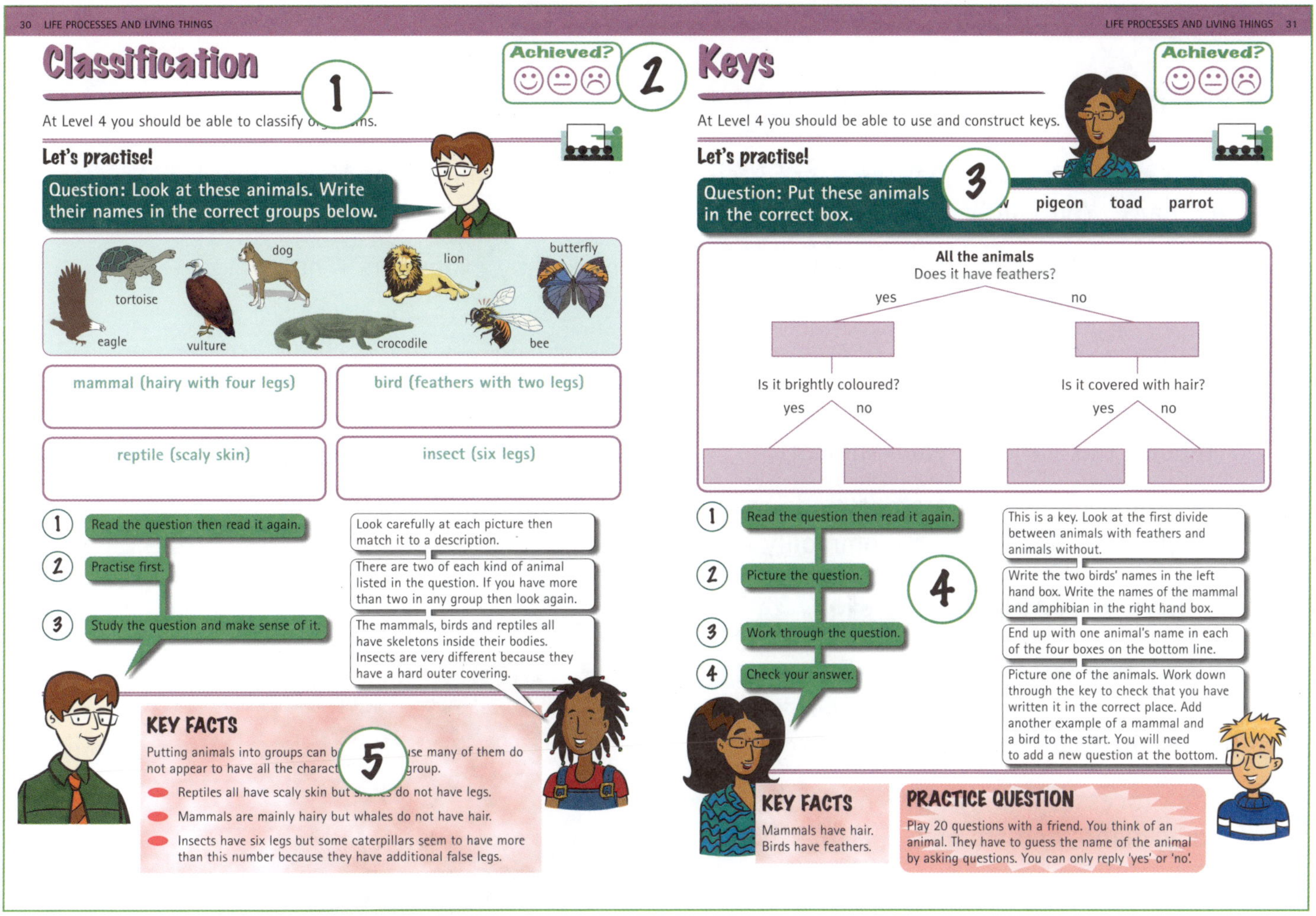

30 LIFE PROCESSES AND LIVING THINGS

Classification

1

Achieved?

2

At Level 4 you should be able to classify o… …ms.

Let's practise!

Question: Look at these animals. Write their names in the correct groups below.

tortoise, dog, lion, butterfly, eagle, vulture, crocodile, bee

mammal (hairy with four legs)

bird (feathers with two legs)

reptile (scaly skin)

insect (six legs)

1. Read the question then read it again.
2. Practise first.
3. Study the question and make sense of it.

Look carefully at each picture then match it to a description.

There are two of each kind of animal listed in the question. If you have more than two in any group then look again.

The mammals, birds and reptiles all have skeletons inside their bodies. Insects are very different because they have a hard outer covering.

KEY FACTS

5

Putting animals into groups can b… …se many of them do not appear to have all the charact… …group.

- Reptiles all have scaly skin but s… do not have legs.
- Mammals are mainly hairy but whales do not have hair.
- Insects have six legs but some caterpillars seem to have more than this number because they have additional false legs.

LIFE PROCESSES AND LIVING THINGS 31

Keys

Achieved?

At Level 4 you should be able to use and construct keys.

Let's practise!

Question: Put these animals in the correct box.

3

…w pigeon toad parrot

All the animals
Does it have feathers?
yes / no
Is it brightly coloured? yes / no
Is it covered with hair? yes / no

1. Read the question then read it again.
2. Picture the question.
3. Work through the question.
4. Check your answer.

4

This is a key. Look at the first divide between animals with feathers and animals without.

Write the two birds' names in the left hand box. Write the names of the mammal and amphibian in the right hand box.

End up with one animal's name in each of the four boxes on the bottom line.

Picture one of the animals. Work down through the key to check that you have written it in the correct place. Add another example of a mammal and a bird to the start. You will need to add a new question at the bottom.

KEY FACTS

Mammals have hair.
Birds have feathers.

PRACTICE QUESTION

Play 20 questions with a friend. You think of an animal. They have to guess the name of the animal by asking questions. You can only reply 'yes' or 'no'.

The National Tests

Key Facts

- The Key Stage 2 National Tests (or SATs) take place in the middle of May in Year 6. You will be tested on Maths, English and Science.
- The tests take place in your school and will be marked by examiners – not your teacher!
- You will get your results in July, two months after you take the tests.
- Most children will get a Level 4 or above, with about 30% getting to Level 5 (though this varies in each subject).
- Individual test scores are not made public but a school's combined scores are published in what are commonly known as league tables.

The Science National Tests

You will take two tests in Science, each one lasting 45 minutes. These are designed to test your knowledge and skills across the following areas of Science:

- Life processes and living things – the human body, plants and animals and their habitats.
- Materials and their properties – changing different materials, understanding the characteristics of different materials.
- Physical processes – electricity, forces, light and sound, the Sun and the Earth.
- Scientific enquiry – ideas and evidence about Science and investigative skills.

DON'T FORGET!

Scientific Enquiry – The National Tests now include more questions that test your *Scientific Enquiry* skills.

The questions will often be based around a picture or a description of an investigation that children have carried out, along with their results. You won't need to carry out the investigation in the test but you might be asked how you would improve it if you were doing the investigation in class.

Recent National Tests papers included questions like:

- Work out the question that the children were investigating.
- Choose the best equipment to use in an investigation.
- Complete a table of results from an investigation.
- Draw conclusions from the results of investigations.
- Answer questions about graphs and charts completed in an investigation.
- Describe what the children have found out from an investigation.

You might also have to answer some questions about a famous scientist! In 2003 there was a series of questions about Edward Jenner. He found a cure for smallpox a long time ago and saved millions of lives!

ACHIEVE LEVEL 4

Test tips and technique

Before the test

1. When you revise, try revising a 'little and often' rather than in long sessions.
2. Learn the Key Facts (at the end of the book) so that you can recall them instantly. These are your tools for performing your calculations.
3. Revise with a friend. You can encourage and learn from each other.
4. Get a good night's sleep the night before.
5. Make sure you have breakfast!
6. Be prepared – bring your own pens and pencils and wear a watch to check the time as you go.

During the test

1. READ THE QUESTION THEN READ IT AGAIN.
2. If you get stuck, don't linger on the same question – move on! You can come back to it later.
3. Never leave a multiple choice question. Guess if you really can't work out the answer.
4. Check to see how many marks a question is worth. Have you 'earned' those marks with your answer?
5. Check your answers after each question. Does your answer look correct?
6. Underline key words in the question.

7. Be aware of the time. After 20 minutes, check to see how far you have got.
8. Try to leave a couple of minutes at the end to read through what you have written.
9. Don't leave any questions unanswered. In the two minutes you have left yourself at the end, make an educated guess at the questions you really couldn't do.
10. Remember, as long as you have done your best, nobody can ask for more. Only you will know if that is the case.

Things to remember

1. Don't panic! If you see a difficult question, take your time, re-read it and have a go!
2. Check every question and every page to be sure you don't miss any! Some questions will want two answers.
3. If a question is about measuring, always write in the UNIT of MEASUREMENT (e.g. newtons, l, kg).
4. Don't be afraid to ask a teacher for anything you need, such as tracing paper or another pencil.
5. Write neatly – if you want to change an answer, put a line through it and write beside the answer box.
6. Always double-check your answers.
7. Read through the whole paper when you've finished!

Finding answers

Achieved? ☺ 😐 ☹

At Level 3 you will need to be able to put forward your own ideas to answer a question.

Let's practise!

Question: Fran and Jane want to find out which make of ladies' tights stretches the most. Suggest some things they could do to try to find this out.

1. Read the question then read it again.
   - What does it suggest?
2. Think about the problem.
   - Think of some tests to compare the stretchiness. Some tights are thick and other are very thin. Some are coloured and some nearly transparent. How many types would you choose? Would the colour really matter? Would it make a difference if they were new or had been worn and washed?
3. Remember the key facts.
   - You need to measure the length of the tights before and after stretching.
4. Work through the problem.
   - You need to find a way to hang them up so you can put weights in the toe. You need to find a way to attach a spring balance if you want to measure the pull.

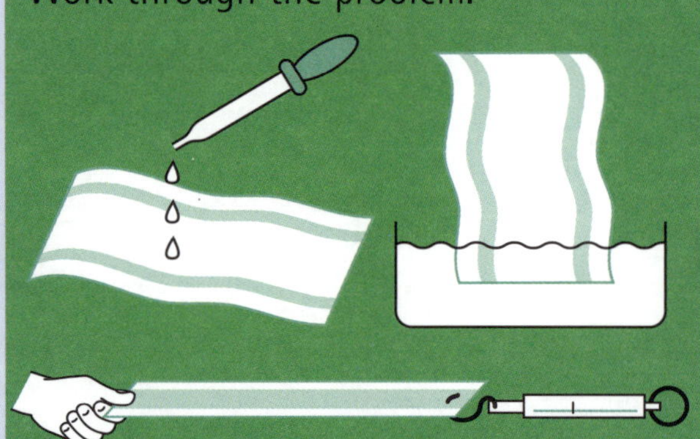

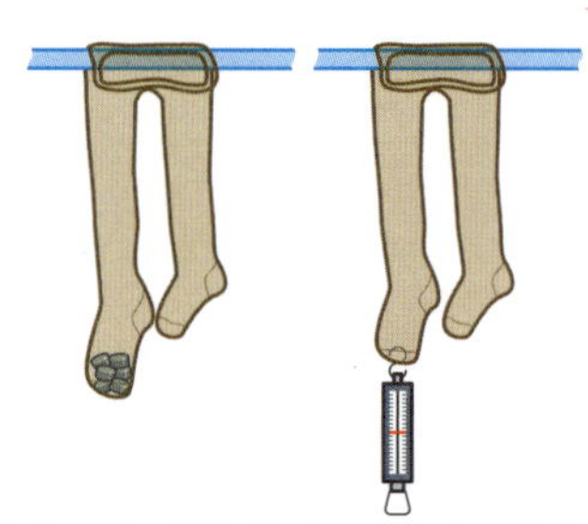

KEY FACTS

Most very stretchy materials are knitted. Use a lens to check the tights.

★ Tip

Test other materials. Cut them into strips all the same size before the test.

Explaining results

Achieved?

At Level 3 you need to be able to explain patterns in results.

Let's practise!

Question: Zac and Kate planted 100 cress seeds. They counted the number of shoots each day.

a) On which day did the first seeds germinate?

b) On which day were there 60 germinated seeds?

c) Do you think there will ever be 100 germinated seeds? Explain your answer.

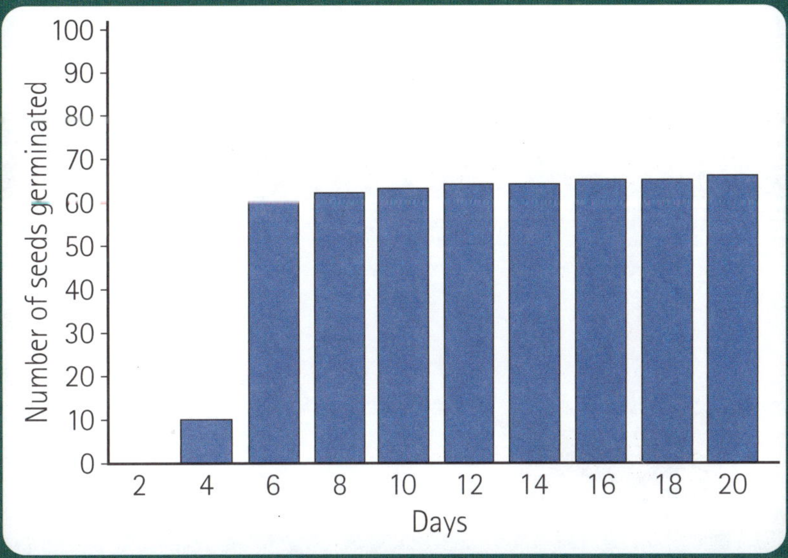

1. Read the question then read it again.
2. Think about the question.
3. Remember the key facts.
4. Work through the problem.

There are three parts to the question. Make sure you answer each part.

The seeds did not germinate until day 4.

The numbers on the vertical axis show the number of seeds that have germinated.

For questions a) and b) look carefully at the chart. Read the number of seedlings on that day. There will probably never be 100 seedlings as not all seeds will sprout.

KEY FACTS

Not all seeds germinate. Some rot and others are not fully formed. Most gardeners plant more seeds than they expect to grow.

Tip

Remember that you are looking at the total number each day.

Use a ruler to help you read the chart more easily.

Living and non-living things

Achieved?

At Level 3 you need to be able to describe the differences between living and non-living things.
For example: the differences between a cuddly toy dog and a real puppy.

Let's practise!

Question: Join each sentence to the correct picture.

CHILD

It can move by itself.

It does not eat.

It breathes.

It will grow into an adult.

It will not grow at all.

DOLL

1. Read the question then read it again.

You are being asked to show the differences between living things and things that are not alive.

2. Remember the key facts.

All living animals can:

- move
- eat
- grow bigger
- reproduce
- breathe
- use their senses
- get rid of waste

3. Work through the problem.

Join up the ones that you are sure about at first. Make sure you only draw one line from each sentence.

KEY FACTS

All living things do the same activities. It is easy to see this in animals. It is much harder to see it in plants.

Tip

Compare a real pet cat with a toy cat.
List what each one can and cannot do.
Repeat with a caterpillar and a wooden toy caterpillar, and a car and a horse.

Factors affecting plant growth

At Level 3 you need to be able to say how changes affect plant growth. For example: this chart shows the effects of being in a different place.

Let's practise!

Question: Harry grew three sunflower plants. She gave them all the same amount of water. She put them in different places.

	Water each day	Place plant kept	Height of plant
Plant A	3 spoons	On windowsill	28 cm
Plant B	3 spoons	In cupboard	15 cm
Plant C	3 spoons	On shady table	21 cm

a) Which plant grew tallest?
b) Which plant was shortest?
c) What was kept the same for each plant?
d) What would be different about the cupboard compared to the windowsill?

1. Read the question then read it again.

   This question has four parts. Look at the table and see what happened to each plant.

2. Think about the question. What does it tell you?

   The last column in the table tells you how big each plant was at the end of the experiment. Everything is the same for each plant except for the place the plant grew in.

3. Remember the key facts.

   Plants need light to grow healthy and strong. They don't grow as well if they are in a shady place.

KEY FACTS

You might get a question where the plants are given different amounts of water.

- Plants with lots of water grow better than plants which are dry.
- However, too much water kills plants.

Grouping materials

Achieved?

At Level 3 you need to be able to group materials according to their properties.

Let's practise!

Question: a) Here are the names of different metals:

wood *brass* *plastic* *steel*

Write the correct material name in each box.

conducts electricity	does not conduct electricity

b) Draw a line from the materials to the correct description.

soap	does not float
copper	
pottery	floats
wax candles	

1. Read the question then read it again.
2. Think about the question. What does it tell you?

In the first part of the question you have to put each material into one group. Each material will go into one group or another. In the second part you must link each material with one description.

The property of the material may be different from the object made from it. For example, steel or glass will float if made into a boat shape.

KEY FACTS

- The two most frequently used magnetic metals are iron and steel. No other common metals are magnetic.
- Wax is light for its size and it floats.
- Soap, copper and pottery are dense for their size and sink.

Tip

You might have to sort materials into groups, such as whether they are magnetic or not. All metals conduct electricity and most non-metals do not conduct electricity.

Uses of materials

Achieved?

At Level 3 you need to be able to say why different materials are used for special purposes.

Let's practise!

Question: Join the name of the material to what it is like. Then join what it is like to what it can be used for. Perspex has been done for you.

Material	What it is like	What it can be used for
perspex	soft and warm	bike tyres
copper	heavy and strong	windows
rubber	see-through	clothes
cotton	conducts electricity	garden walls
stone	bouncy and hard wearing	electrical wires

1 Read the question then read it again.

You have to do two steps. Join the material to what it is like first. Make sure each material is joined to a description. Now join one description to one use.

2 Remember the key facts.

Objects are made from materials. Don't confuse the material's properties with the objects it can be made into. Glass, for instance, can be made into objects that are not see-through! Stone can be light if it is in a small piece.

KEY FACTS

Here are some other materials and their uses.

leather – bends and is strong – belts and shoes
plastic – does not conduct heat – pan handles
plastic – easy to shape – bags
paper – cheap and easy to make into sheets – writing
steel – strong and cheap – food cans
aluminium – strong, light and conducts heat – pans
silk – soft and feels smooth – shirts

Reversible and non-reversible

Achieved?

At Level 3 you need to be able to say which changes can be reversed and which cannot be reversed.

Let's practise!

Question: Draw a line from the change to the correct group. Two have been done for you.

freezing orange juice
burning wood
baking pastry
melting chocolate
burning oil in a lamp
dissolving sugar
making pottery in a kiln

CHANGE WHICH IS REVERSIBLE
CHANGE WHICH IS NOT REVERSIBLE

1. Think about the question. What does it tell you?

You need to match each change with the right description. Think about whether you could easily get the original material back again.

2. Remember the key facts.

Some changes can be reversed easily. These are mainly changes that involve melting, freezing and dissolving.

KEY FACTS

- Freezing liquid is reversible because it can be reversed by warming the ice.
- Burning materials is not reversible because the ash cannot be made back into paper again. Also, material is lost to the air as a gas.
- Baking is not reversible because it is impossible to get a bag of flour, butter or sugar out of the cooked cake.
- Melting solids is reversible because it can be reversed by refreezing the ice cream.
- Burning a candle is not reversible because the gas given off by burning cannot be made into wax again.
- Dissolving a solid is reversible by evaporating the water and leaving the solid behind.
- Heating clay in a kiln is not reversible because even if you break up the pottery you cannot get the clay back again.

Electrical circuits

Achieved?

At Level 3 you need to be able to explain why some electrical circuits work and others do not.

Let's practise!

Question: Explain why each of these circuits does not work:

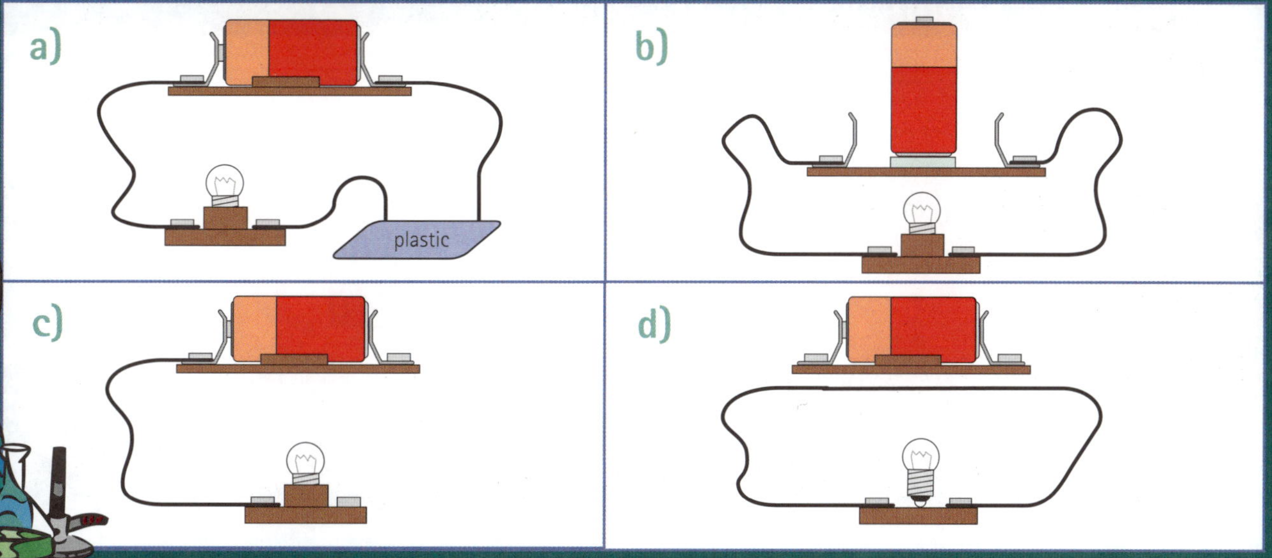

1. Read the question then read it again.

   Each drawing shows a different circuit. The bulb is not lit in any of the circuits. Write an explanation for why each one does not work.

2. Remember the key facts.

   All circuits must have a battery to supply electricity. The bulb has to be connected. All parts of the circuit must be electrical conductors.

3. Work through the problem.

   In a) the electric current cannot flow through the plastic, which is an electrical insulator.

   In b) the electric current cannot flow because the battery is not fitted properly.

   In c) the electric current cannot flow because there is a break in the circuit.

   In d) the bulb will not light because it is not connected to the electric current.

KEY FACTS

- All metals conduct electricity.
- Most non-metals are electrical insulators.
- You need a complete circuit and a power source to make a current flow.

How we see things

Achieved?

At Level 3 you need to be able to explain that we see things when **light from them enters our eyes.**

Let's practise!

Question: Here are three drawings that might help explain how we see things.

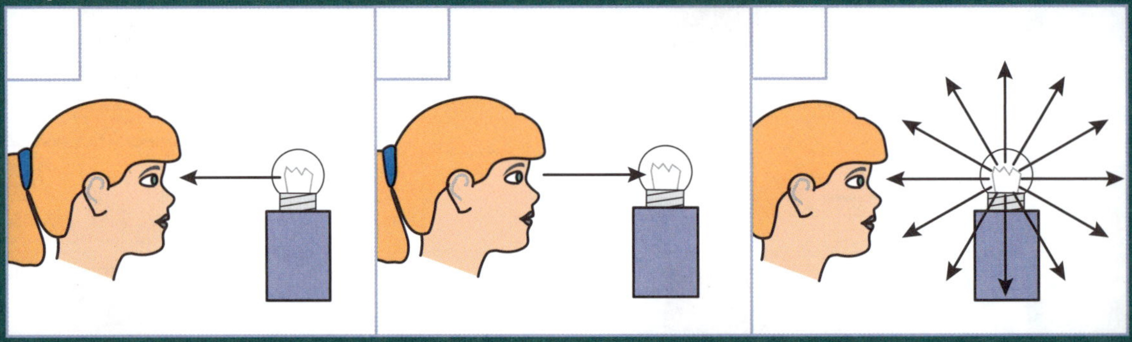

Tick the box next to the diagram you think shows the best way of describing how we see a candle.

1. Think about the question. What does it tell you?

   Each diagram is a way of thinking about how we see a bulb. You have to decide which seems best.

2. Remember the key facts.

   Light travels from sources of light. Light travels away from the source in all directions. Only a small amount of the light produced enters our eyes.

3. Work through the problem.

   - The first idea is correct BUT it only shows one beam of light from the bulb. Is that all the light that is given off?
   - The second idea shows that beams from the eye go to the bulb. This is not correct.
   - The last idea is the best one because it shows light coming off in all directions. Only some of the light goes into the eye of the person looking at the bulb.

KEY FACTS

Light travels from sources such as the Sun, matches, candles, TV and stars. Some of the light they produce goes into our eyes. Most of the light is reflected off other objects and this reflected light also goes into our eyes.

Pushes and pulls

Achieved?

At Level 3 you need to be able to describe the effects of big and small pulls and pushes.

Let's practise!

Question: Pulls are needed to move objects. Put these pulls in order from largest to smallest. Write in 1 next to the biggest pull and 4 next to the smallest.

Pushes are needed to move objects. Put these pushes in order from largest to smallest. Write in 1 next to the biggest push and 4 next to the smallest.

1. Read the question then read it again.
2. Remember the key facts.

There are four pushes and four pulls. Start with the biggest and then the smallest – these are easiest.

Small objects give small pushes and pulls. Large objects give big pushes and pulls.

Tip

Pushes and pulls can also happen even when objects are not touching. Magnets can pull (attract) or push (repel). Gravity is just a pull force.

Patterns in data

Achieved?

At Level 4 you will be asked to spot patterns in data.
For example: interpreting a bar chart.

Let's practise!

Question: This chart shows the number of plants found in grassy places.

Where are most plants found?

Where are the fewest plants found? There are two places.

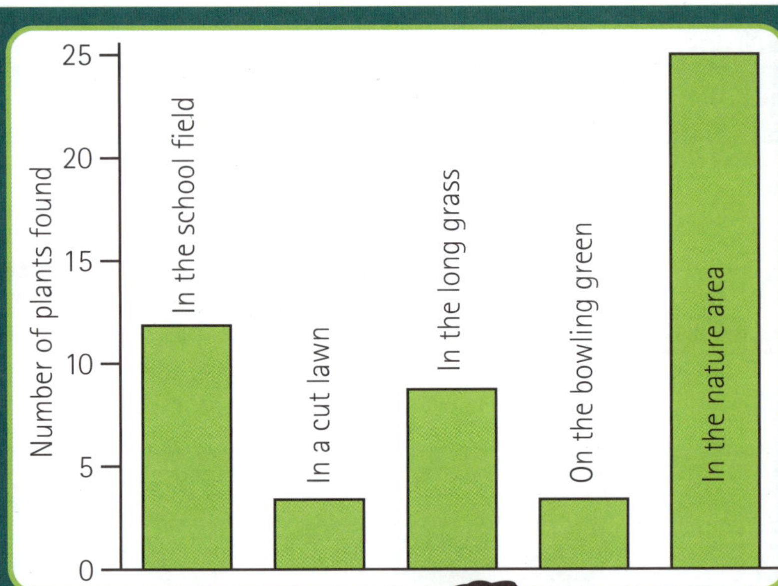

1. Read the question then read it again.
2. Picture the question. What does it tell you?
3. Remember the key facts.

You are only being asked to say what the chart shows.

The place is along the bottom and the number of plants up the side.

The taller columns show more plants.

KEY FACTS

There are two main sorts of graphs and charts that could show this kind of information.

Bar chart

The taller the column, the greater the amount.

Pie chart

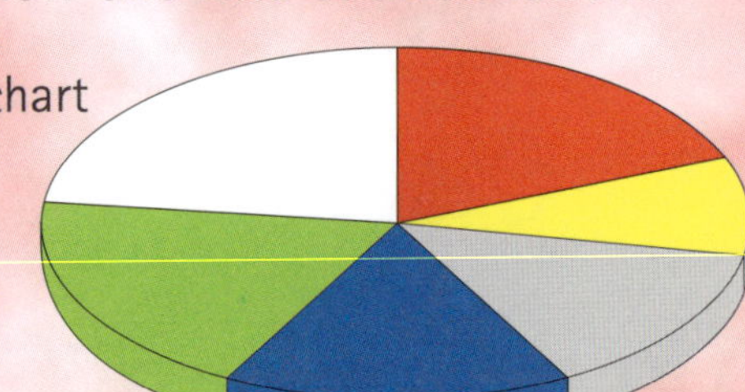

The bigger the piece of pie, the greater the amount.

Explaining patterns in data

Achieved?

At Level 4 you will be asked to explain patterns in data.
For example: saying that one factor depends on another.

Let's practise!

Question: Look at this chart. It shows how far a toy car rolled down a ramp onto a carpet. The height of the ramp above the carpet was changed. Explain the pattern you see in the chart.

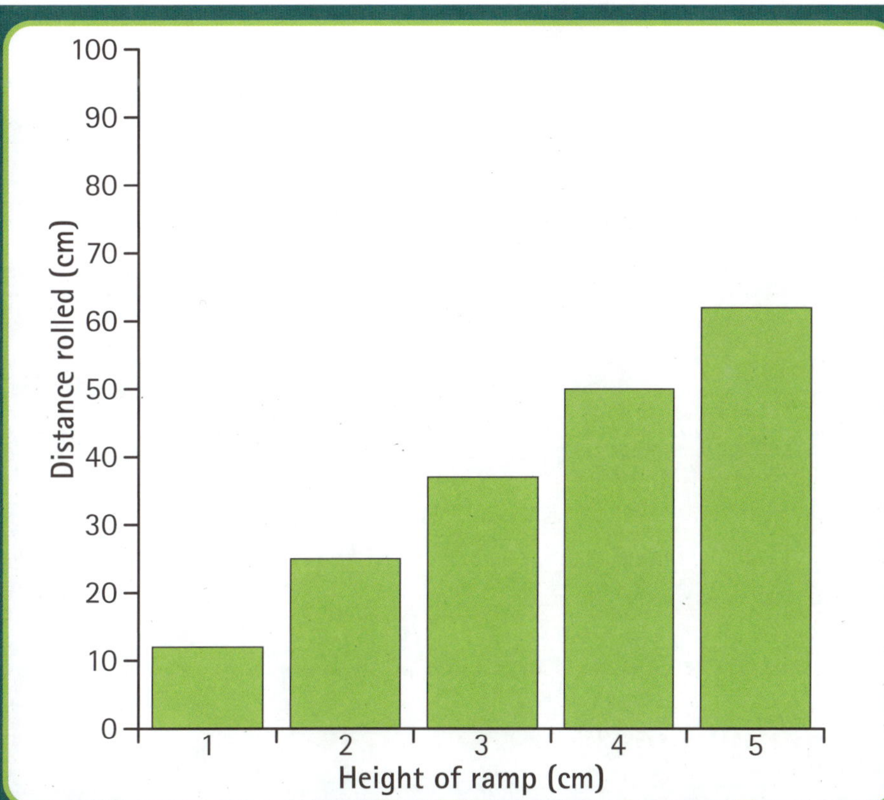

1. Read the question then read it again.
2. Picture the question. What does it tell you?
3. Remember the key facts.
4. Work through the problem.

This time you are being asked to explain the chart and not simply describe it.

Five heights of ramp were tried.

The higher the ramp, the further the toy rolled.

The toy rolled further as the height of the ramp was increased. The distance travelled depended on the height of the ramp.
Will this pattern continue if we keep making the ramp higher?

Tip

Look for the easy patterns and describe them first.

Making predictions

Achieved?

At Level 4, before you start an experiment, you will be asked to think about what will happen and predict the results.

Let's practise!

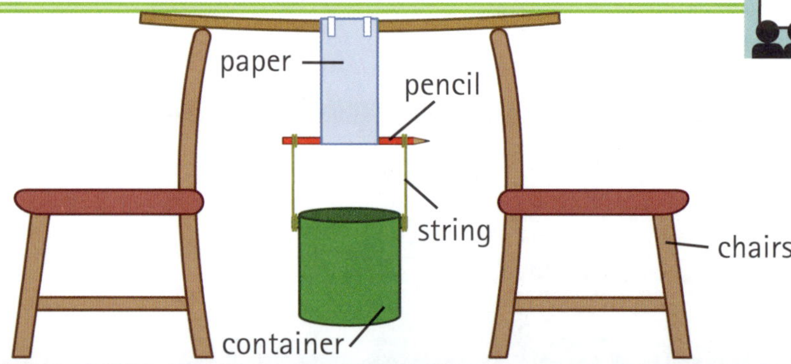

Question: Paul is testing the strength of different strips of paper. Paul's teacher asks him to predict which one will be strongest.

a) What factors do you think he should think about? Tick two boxes.

- The thickness of the string. ☐
- The colour of the paper. ☐
- The width of the paper strip. ☐
- The length of the strip. ☐

b) He has to decide which masses to get out of the cupboard. Tick the box that shows the best set of masses to test the paper's strength.

- 1 gram masses ☐
- 10 gram masses ☐
- 1 kg masses ☐
- 10 kg masses ☐

1. Read the question then read it again.
   There are two parts to the question. Only tick two boxes in the first part and one in the second.
2. Picture the question. What does it tell you?
   You will be testing the paper to see how much weight it can carry.
3. Remember the key facts.
   The factors that will affect the strength of the paper are the way it is made and the thickness of the paper.
4. Work through the problem.
   Explain why you have chosen to tick these boxes.

Questions in an experiment

Achieved?

At Level 4 you will have to decide which questions to investigate.

Let's practise!

Question: Pat is testing different size parachutes.
She made all the parachutes from the same type of plastic.

a) Which question was she investigating?
Tick the correct box.

- ☐ Do heavy parachutes fall more slowly?
- ☐ Do large parachutes fall more slowly than smaller ones?
- ☐ Do plastic parachutes fall more slowly than paper ones?
- ☐ Do red parachutes fall more slowly than yellow ones?

b) This table shows the results of her test.

Area of the parachute	100 cm^2	200 cm^2	250 cm^2
Time taken to fall	1 second	2 seconds	2.5 seconds

Explain the pattern you can see.

1. Read the question then read it again.
2. Picture the question. What does it tell you?
3. What is similar in everyday life?

There are two parts. In the first part you have to decide what she wanted to find out. In the second part you have to use her table of results.

She kept everything the same apart from the size of the parachute canopy.

If you jumped out of a plane you would not want to have a parachute the size of an umbrella. You would want a large parachute!

Making sense of graphs

Achieved?

At Level 4 you will have to spot patterns in graphs.

Let's practise!

Question: Ravi tested how long it took sugar to dissolve in water at different temperatures.
Here is the graph he made.
Use the graph to help.

a) How long did it take for the sugar to dissolve in water at 30 °C?

b) How long did it take the sugar to dissolve in water at 40 °C?

c) Explain the pattern you can see in this graph.

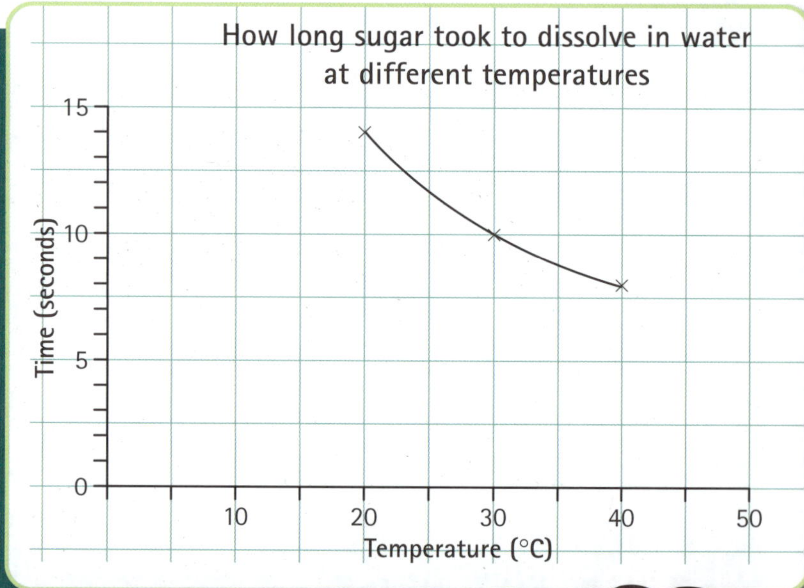

1 Read the question then read it again.

In the first two questions simply look at the crosses on the graph.
The third question needs thinking about more carefully.

2 Remember the key facts.

On a line graph you have to know where to look.

The vertical axis shows how long it took the sugar to dissolve.

The horizontal axis is the line along the bottom, which shows the temperature of the water.

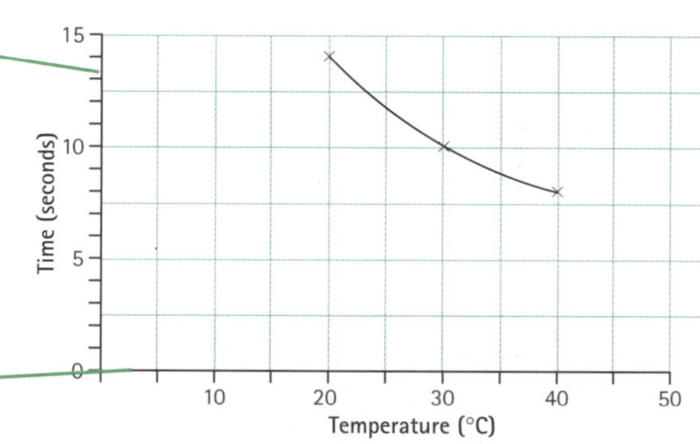

3 What is similar in everyday life?

Common sense tells you that sugar dissolves more quickly in warm water than it does in cooler water. If your answers do not show this pattern then look again.

Plotting line graphs

Achieved?

At Level 4 you will be asked to plot line graphs.

Let's practise!

Question: Sophie was testing gyrocopters to see how quickly they fell. She attached different masses and timed how quickly each fell.

Mass on gyrocopter	5 g	10 g	15 g
Time taken to fall	4 seconds	3 seconds	2 seconds

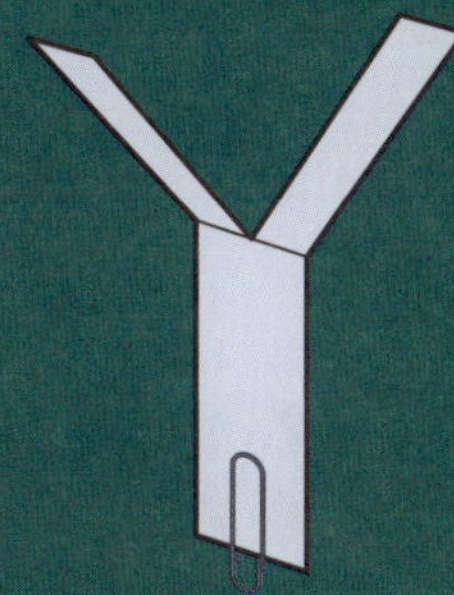

Mark the three results on the graph paper.
Join up the marks to make a line graph.

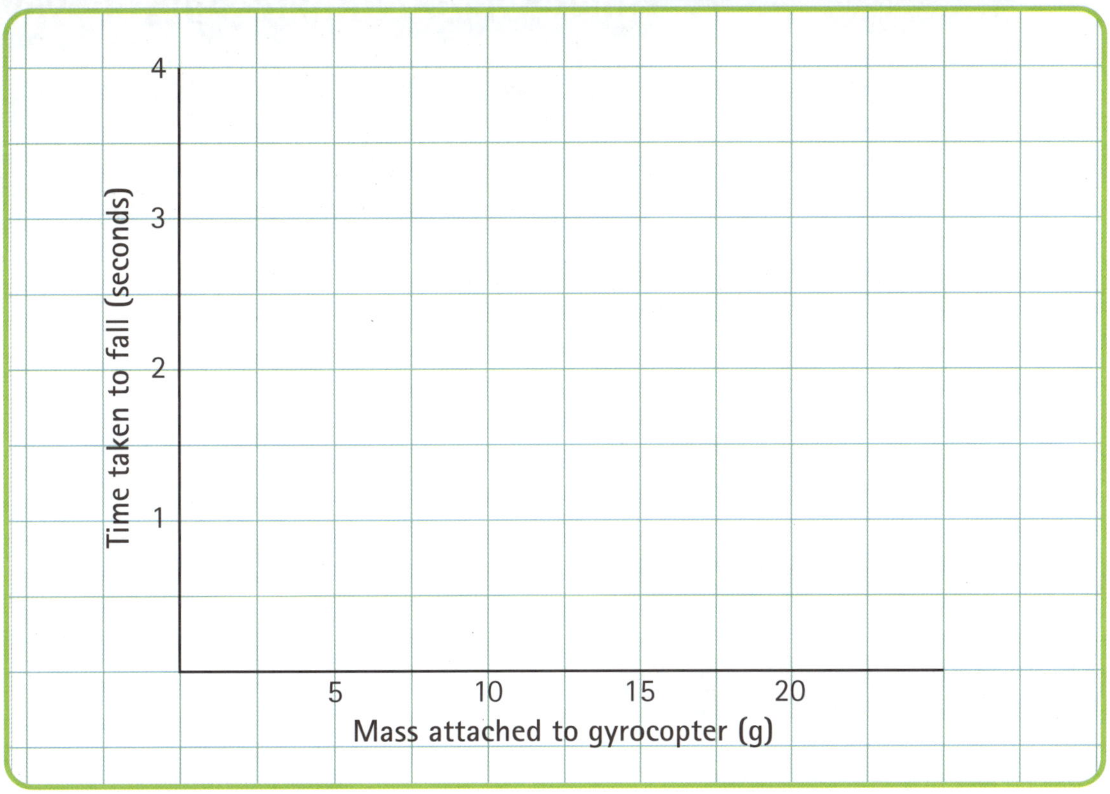

1. Read the question then read it again.
2. Picture the question. What does it tell you?
3. Work through the problem.

You have to make three marks on the graph paper. Start by looking at the bottom axis and find 5g. Go up until you reach 4 seconds. Make a mark.

Heavier gyrocopters fall faster than light gyrocopters.

Join the marks to make a line graph.

Roots, stems and water

Achieved?

At Level 4 you need to be able to say how different parts of plants work.
For example: all plants need water. Water is drawn up from the roots and travels to all parts of the plant through the stem.

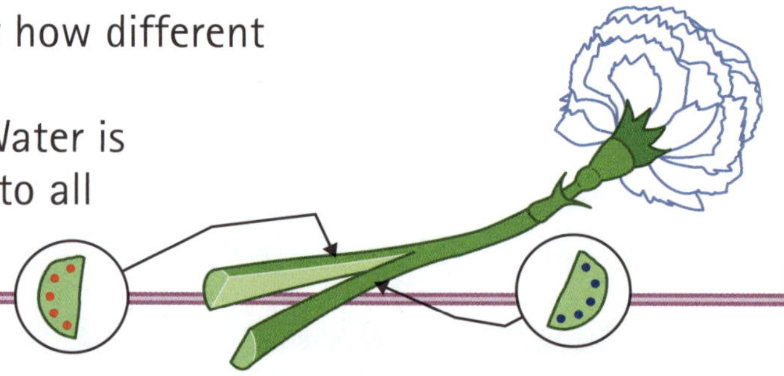

Let's practise!

Question: Jim put some blue ink in a glass of water. He put red ink in another glass. He split the stem of a carnation almost in half. He put one part of the stem into the red water and the other part into the blue water. After an hour there were red marks all the way up one part of the carnation and blue marks in the other part.

Why do you think there were red and blue marks on the carnation flower?

1. Read the question then read it again.

   The carnation was white before it went into the water and now it has red and blue marks in the long thin tubes in its stem and the flower.

2. Picture the experiment.

   Imagine a carnation in clear water. Would the flower have become coloured?

3. Remember the key facts.

   Water moves from the roots to all parts of the plant.

4. Work through the problem.

   The ink must have travelled up the stem.

5. Check your answer.

   What do you think would happen if you put celery sticks in coloured water? After a few hours the coloured water begins to move up the stems.

KEY FACTS

water – all living things need it
stems – water travels up stems from roots
roots – take water from the soil
leaves and flowers – need water, which travels up to them

Tip

In most plants water travels through tiny tubes. It travels from roots, up the stem or trunk and evaporates from the leaves.

Flower parts

Achieved?

At Level 4 you should be able to name the different parts of a flower.

Let's practise!

Question: This diagram shows the different parts of the flower. Use the words below to label the diagram correctly.

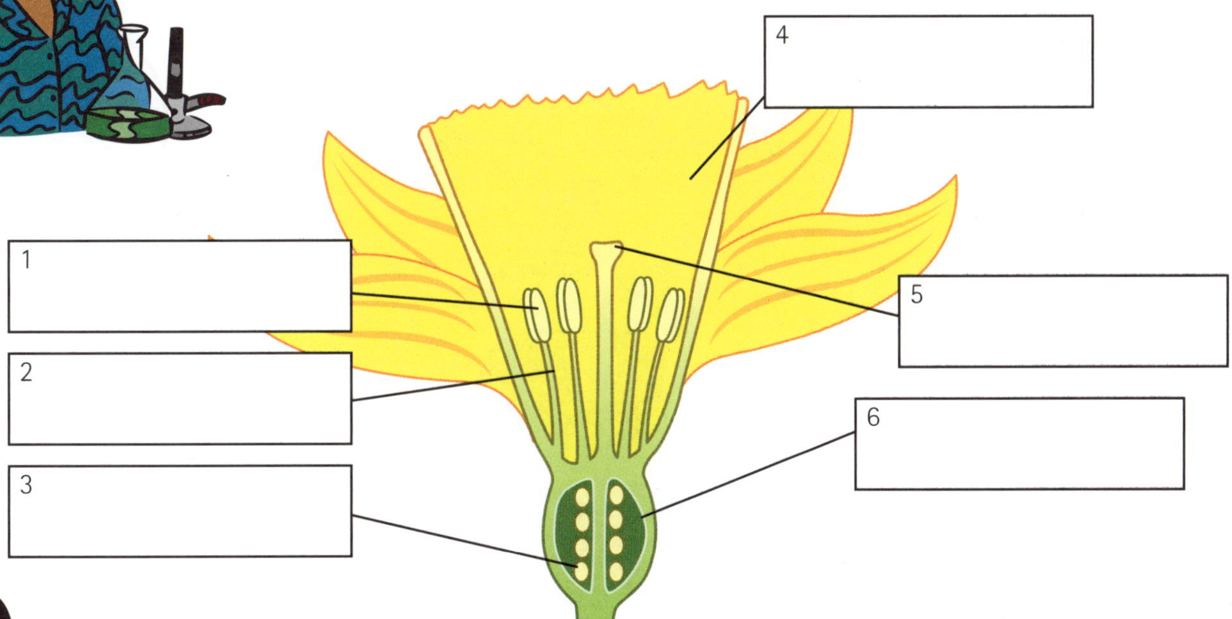

stigma ovule stamen ovary petal anther

1. Read the question then read it again.
2. Practise first.
3. Study the question and make sense of it.
4. Study diagrams of different flower types.

Simply name the parts and match the number to the correct word.

Jot down the numbers and write the parts next to each number.

Label the parts you do know first then think about those you are not sure about.

Most flowers have the same sort of parts.

KEY FACTS

stigma – top of the female part of the flower

stamen – the male parts, which produce pollen

ovary – the seed box

ovule – the undeveloped seed

petals – colourful outer part of the flower

anther – end of the stamen where pollen is found

Tip

staMEN – (male)

stigMA – (female – as in 'mum'!)

Human organs

Achieved?

At Level 4 you should be able to name some of the organs of the human body.

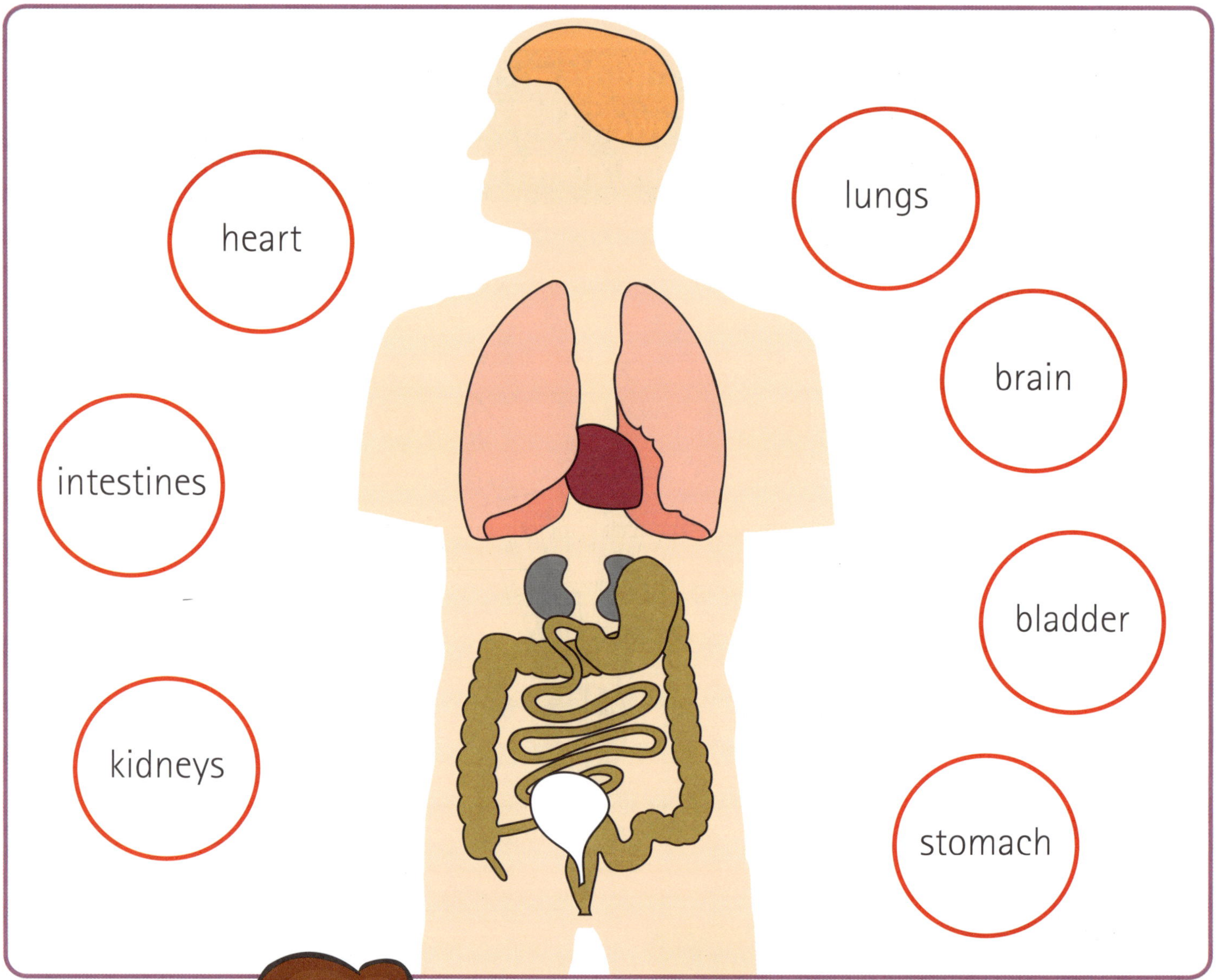

Let's practise!

Question: Draw a line from each word to the correct organ.

1. Read the question then read it again.
2. Look carefully.
3. Study the question and make sense of it.

Look at the diagram before drawing any lines.

Lungs, heart and stomach are all very close. There are two lungs, and the stomach is lower down than the heart.

The stomach is connected to the intestines. The kidneys are connected to the bladder.

Living processes

Achieved?

At Level 4 you should be able to show your understanding of living things.

Let's practise!

Question: Which of these is the odd one out? cardboard box, fish, badger.

How do you know that plants are alive?

List as many reasons as you can.

1. Read the question then read it again.
2. Remember key facts.
3. Work through the problem.

Write some reasons for plants being alive.

We know that animals are alive because they move, have babies, have senses like eyesight or hearing, they grow, breathe, get rid of waste like urine and they eat.

Plants are more difficult. They produce seeds, they grow, and they use sunlight, water and air to make food.

Plants go through all the same life processes as animals but as they do them slowly we might not notice it. Plant leaves turn slowly to catch as much sunlight as they can. They do not breathe in the way that animals like us do but they take in air and give out waste gases through their leaves.

KEY FACTS

All living things can:

- move (even if very slowly)
- take in one gas and give out a different one
- sense things in the environment (smell, see)
- grow
- reproduce (have babies or produce seeds)
- get rid of waste materials
- feed

Classification

Achieved?

At Level 4 you should be able to classify organisms.

Let's practise!

Question: Look at these animals. Write their names in the correct groups below.

mammal (hairy with four legs)	bird (feathers with two legs)
reptile (scaly skin)	**insect (six legs)**

1. Read the question then read it again.
2. Practise first.
3. Study the question and make sense of it.

Look carefully at each picture then match it to a description.

There are two of each kind of animal listed in the question. If you have more than two in any group then look again.

The mammals, birds and reptiles all have skeletons inside their bodies. Insects are very different because they have a hard outer covering.

KEY FACTS

Putting animals into groups can be hard because many of them do not appear to have all the characters of their group.

- Reptiles all have scaly skin but snakes do not have legs.
- Mammals are mainly hairy but whales do not have hair.
- Insects have six legs but some caterpillars seem to have more than this number because they have additional false legs.

Keys

Achieved?

At Level 4 you should be able to use and construct keys.

Let's practise!

Question: Put these animals in the correct box.

cow pigeon toad parrot

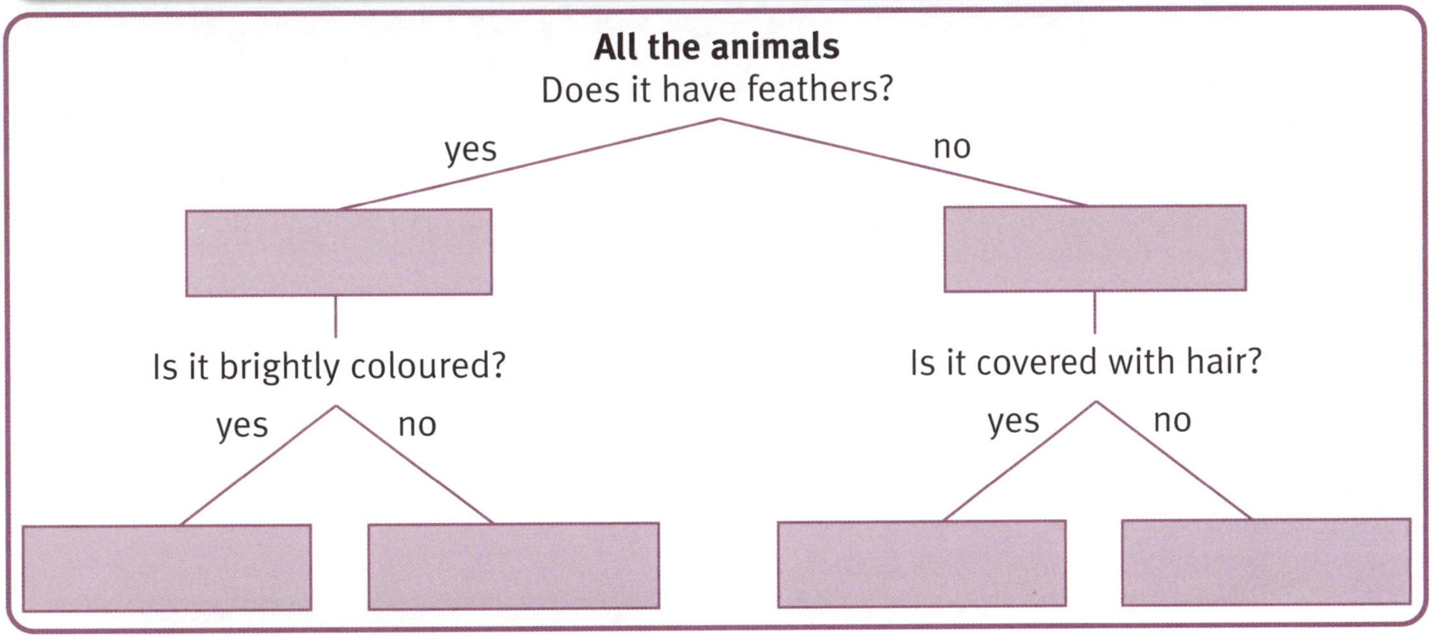

1. Read the question then read it again.

   This is a key. Look at the first divide between animals with feathers and animals without.

2. Picture the question.

   Write the two birds' names in the left hand box. Write the names of the mammal and amphibian in the right hand box.

3. Work through the question.

   End up with one animal's name in each of the four boxes on the bottom line.

4. Check your answer.

   Picture one of the animals. Work down through the key to check that you have written it in the correct place. Add another example of a mammal and a bird to the start. You will need to add a new question at the bottom.

KEY FACTS

Mammals have hair.
Birds have feathers.

PRACTICE QUESTION

Play 20 questions with a friend. You think of an animal. They have to guess the name of the animal by asking questions. You can only reply 'yes' or 'no'.

Animals in their environment

Achieved?

At Level 4 you should be able to say how animals are adapted to their environment.

Let's practise!

Question: Draw a line from the animal to where it lives. Connect where it lives to the adaptation.

Animal	Where it lives	Adaptation
shark	grasslands	streamlined body to swim fast
penguin	grasslands	thick coat of feathers to keep warm
worm	on icy land and in cold sea	long legs to run and horns to defend
antelope	in the soil	strong claws and teeth
lion	in oceans	long, trim body

1. Read the question then read it again.
2. Practise first.
3. Study the question and make sense of it.

There are two main parts to this question. In each part there are five lines to draw.

Draw the line in pencil first. There are two animals that live in grasslands.

Think about the adaptation and the way it helps the animal to survive. For instance, the shark needs a streamlined body to help it swim quickly.

KEY FACTS

The place where an animal lives is called its **habitat**.

Predators and prey

Achieved?

At Level 4 you should be able to talk about food chains.

Let's practise!

Question: Draw an arrow from the prey to the predator.

PREY

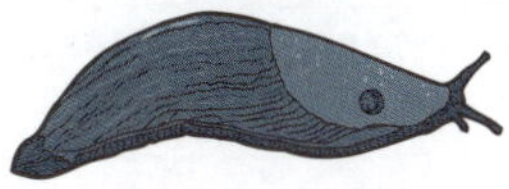
slug

antelope

caribou

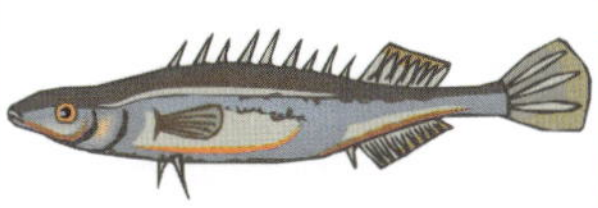
stickleback

seal

PREDATOR

killer whale

pike

hedgehog

cheetah

wolf

1. Read the question then read it again.

In this question you should try to connect each predator to its prey.

2. Picture the question.

Prey are animals that are eaten. **Predators** are animals that eat other animals. The arrow means 'is eaten by'.

3. Remember the key facts.

Prey are the animals that are eaten by predators. Some prey are predators of smaller animals themselves. Seals, for instance, will eat fish. The arrows are always drawn **towards** the predator.

Human food chains

Achieved?

At Level 4 you should be able to describe food chains.

Let's practise!

Question: This is the food chain for lamb.
All food chains start with the Sun.

Sun ⟶ grass ⟶ lamb ⟶ human

Draw the arrows into this food chain.

Sun [ ] wheat [ ] chicken [ ] human

Write in the missing word in this food chain.

Sun ⟶ [ ] ⟶ cow ⟶ human

Draw your own food chain for orange juice. Start with the Sun.

1. Read the question then read it again. — This question has several parts.
2. Remember the key facts. — A food chain shows which animals eat other animals and plants. The arrow points to the animal which is eating (the predator).
3. Study the question and make sense of it. — Each food chain starts with the Sun. This is the main source of energy. All these food chains end with a person. We are the top predator on the planet. It is fairly rare for another animal to kill and eat a human, although it does happen.

Tip

It does not matter that we do not the eat the animal itself. If we drink milk from a cow or eat the egg of a chicken then we draw the food chain as if we ate the animal itself.

Classifying animals

Achieved?

At Level 4 you should be able to group animals based on their features.

Let's practise!

Question: Here are three different land animals.
Which group of animals do they belong in?
Choose mammal, insect or bird.
Give one reason for each.

The turkey is in the ________ group because it ________

The beetle is in the ________ group because it ________

The mole is in the ________ group because it ________

Here are three animals.
Choose fish, reptile or mammal.

The shark is in the ________ group because it ________

The snake is in the ________ group because it ________

The rabbit is in the ________ group because it ________

1. Read the question then read it again.
2. Study the question and make sense of it.
3. Remember the key facts.

In each question pick out the one you know first. This makes it easier to decide for the other two.

There are two parts to each question. Start by deciding which group the animals belong to. Then write in a reason why it is in that group.

Insects are easy – they have six legs.
Mammals have hair and feed their young on milk.
Reptiles lay eggs and have a scaly body.
Birds are easy – they have feathers.
Fish have fins, gills and scaly skin.

Thermal insulators and conductors

Achieved?

At Level 4 you are expected to know that heat passes through some materials more easily than through others. For example: heat travels more easily through metals than it does through plastic and wood.

Let's practise!

Experiment: Jo has filled three cups with hot tea. One cup is polystyrene, one is pottery and one is metal.

- The metal cup feels hot.
- The pottery cup feels warm.
- The polystyrene cup is only slightly warm.

Explain the difference that Jo has felt.

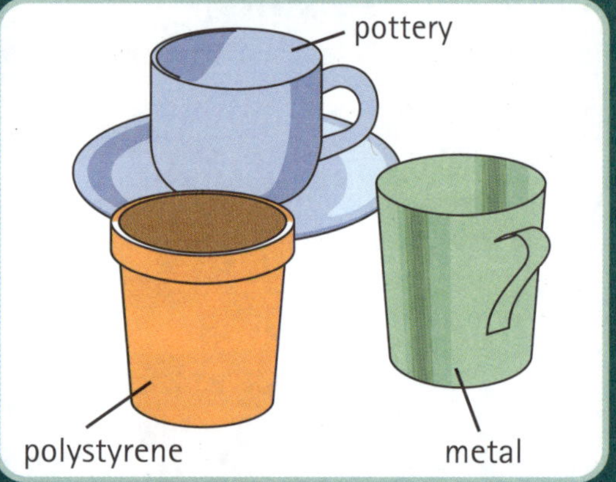

1. Read the question then read it again. — Why is one cup hotter than the others?
2. Picture the question. What does it tell you? — The heat must have come from the hot water.
3. Think about real life examples. — Kettles and pans have plastic or wooden handles to make them easy to touch. Oven gloves help to stop the heat travelling from very hot objects.
4. Remember the key facts. — Heat travels through materials.
5. Work through the problem. — Heat must travel through the metal and pottery. If it can travel easily through a material, then that material is a good conductor.

KEY FACTS

material – what objects are made from
metals – good conductors of heat
pottery – fairly good conductor of heat
wood and **polystyrene** – very poor conductors of heat (also called insulators)

Check your answer

A conductor of electricity lets electricity through... so, using the same sort of words... a conductor of heat lets heat through.

Good conductors let heat through more easily than poor conductors.

Gases

Achieved?

At Level 4 you should know there are many types of gas. For example: air is a mixture of gases. Carbon dioxide, helium and water vapour are gases.

Let's practise!

Question: Spot the gases in this:

Jo goes to the fair. People are holding balloons that float in the air. A hot-air balloon takes off from a field. Jo drinks a fizzy drink and the bubbles tickle her nose. The man selling hotdogs heats them using bottled gas. You can smell the cooking from a long way off.

1. Read the question then read it again.

   Did you spot the gases? There were four gases in the writing.

2. Picture the question. What does it tell you?

   We use gases all the time.

3. Remember the key facts.

   Materials can be either gas, liquid or solid. This question is about gases.

4. Think of everyday examples.

   Air is a mixture of gases.
   Helium is used to fill airships and balloons.
   Carbon dioxide is the gas we breathe out and we use to make drinks fizzy.
   Natural gas is the gas we burn in gas cookers.

KEY FACTS

Air is a mixture that includes nitrogen, oxygen, water vapour and carbon dioxide.

Helium is a very light gas so it floats in air.

Carbon dioxide dissolves in water to make drinks fizzy.

Natural gas burns easily.

Remember:

Gases are everywhere. We breathe them all the time.

- Some come out of car exhausts.
- Divers breathe air in tanks when underwater.
- Astronauts take air with them into space.

Grouping materials

Achieved?

At Level 4 you will need to be able to classify materials.

Let's practise!

Question: Harry found four kinds of paper. He put them into a branching key. Write the names into each box. The first one has been completed.

card sugar paper
tissue greaseproof

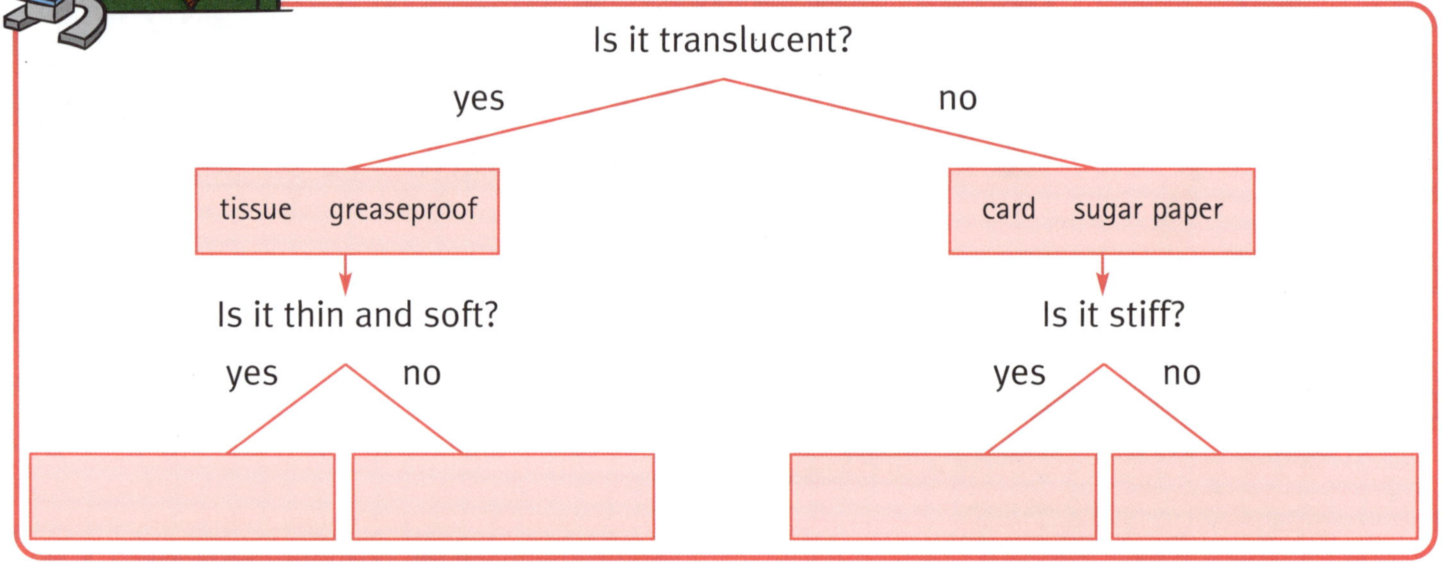

1. Read the question then read it again.
2. Picture the question. What does it tell you?
3. Make up a branching key of your own.

This is just like the branching key you use to classify animals.

Look at the way the materials are divided by the questions.

Make up your own branching key with other materials and different properties, e.g. 'paper' and 'strength'.

Tip

Branching keys can be used to classify animals as well as materials.

KEY FACTS

Translucent – materials let light pass through, but you cannot see details.

Separating mixtures

Achieved?

At Level 4 you will need to know about the ways to separate simple mixtures.

Let's practise!

Question: Ali made a solution of salt and water. After a few minutes stirring she could no longer see the salt. She left it in a saucer on the radiator overnight. Next day the water had gone and she was left with the salt in the saucer. What happened to the salt and water when she stirred it? What happened to the water overnight?

1. Read the question then read it again.
2. Picture the question. What does it tell you?
3. Remember the key facts.
4. Work through the problem.

This solution is a mixture of salt and water. To get the solid salt back Ali has to get rid of the water.

If you pour a solution of salt and water through a sieve nothing useful happens. The solution simply goes through the sieve.

Salt dissolves in water. If you let the water evaporate the salt will be left behind.

If you did this in the classroom you would:

- dissolve the salt in some water
- let the water evaporate
- collect the salt.

KEY FACTS

dissolve – you cannot see the solid at all because it is in tiny particles in water

solution – a mixture where a solid has dissolved in a liquid

evaporate – this happens when a liquid turns to a gas. This leaves behind any solid that was dissolved

Ways to separate mixtures

sieve – use this to separate most **undissolved** solids from a liquid, or to separate two solids of different size

filter – use this to separate a **solution** from undissolved solids

Making mixtures

Achieved?

At Level 4 you should be able to describe the changes that occur when materials are mixed. For example: you should be able to describe ways to speed up dissolving.

Let's practise!

Question: Tim made four mixtures with water.

☐	salt	after a minute the mixture was see-through
☐	gravel	all the gravel sank to the bottom
☐	cocoa	the mixture was cloudy
☐	instant tea	the mixture was see-through and brown coloured

Tick the boxes of those mixtures that dissolved.

Tim then tried different ways to make them dissolve more quickly. Tick the things that helped the powders dissolve more quickly.

- stir the mixture ☐
- use more water ☐
- use hot water ☐
- use more solid ☐

1. Read the question then read it again.
   In the first part all the information is in the question. In the second part (how to speed up dissolving) you have to rely on what you already know.
2. Remember the key facts.
   When a mixture **dissolves** in water you can no longer see it. It leaves the water **transparent** (see-through). Sometimes the water can be coloured. Fizzy drinks have colour dissolved in them.
3. Work through the problem to make sense of the information.
   Things to speed dissolving are **stirring** and using **warm water**. Try this at home or in school.

Solid, liquid and gas

Achieved?

At Level 4 you will need to know that materials can be solid, liquid or gas.

Let's practise!

Question: Write the name of each of these materials in the correct column.

stone oxygen volcanic lava
paper milk shampoo
helium chocolate hydrogen
ice cream oil

Solid at room temperature	Liquid at room temperature	Gas at room temperature

Think about your breakfast. Can you name two materials that are solid? Name two that are liquid. Are there any gases?

1. Read the question then read it again.
2. Remember the key facts.

Write the name of the material in the correct column. When it comes to the breakfast question, cereals, sugar and milk are a good starting point.

- Solids will not run and can be cut into pieces.
- Liquids are runny but stay in a container or on a surface.
- Gas escapes to fill any container.

Tip

Some liquids, like shampoo, run slowly.

Evaporation

Achieved?

At Level 4 you need to know about the factors that affect the way liquids evaporate.

Let's practise!

Question: Kamal wanted to check if the place a container was kept made a difference to the speed at which water in it evaporated.

He put 100 ml of water into three different containers.

He left one container on a sunny windowsill for two days. He put another in a warm cupboard. The third went in the fridge.

From which container did the water evaporate most quickly/ least quickly?

Why was there this difference?

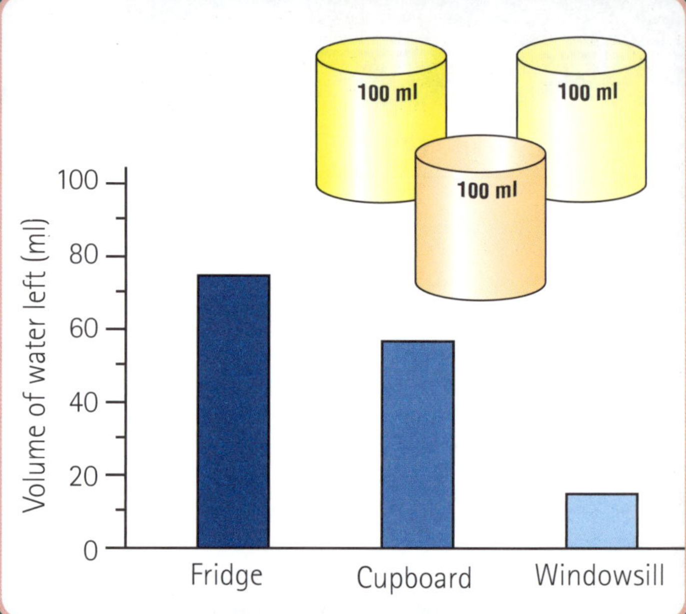

1. Read the question then read it again.

The question assumes you know that water evaporates. This happens when water from the surface changes to a **gas**. There seems to be a difference between the way water **evaporates** in different places. You are asked to spot the differences from the bar chart and then explain the difference.

2. Picture the question. What does it tell you?

Water evaporates at a different rate from one container compared with another.

3. Remember the key facts.

Water will evaporate more quickly from a container in a warm place. If there is a top to the container, water vapour may not be able to escape at all.

Tip 1

If you do this experiment in the classroom, try to make sure the containers have the same amount of water.

Tip 2

A 'factor' is something you can change.

Sieving and filtering

At Level 4 you will need to know about ways to separate mixtures.

Let's practise!

Question: Kelly's mum wants to get the stones out of the soil before sowing seeds. What should she do?

Bill's dad changes the filter on the vacuum cleaner. Why does he do this?

1. Read the question then read it again.
2. Picture the question. What does it tell you?
3. Think of other examples.

There are two parts to this one but both use the same method of separating the mixture.

These are both everyday events.

To remove the stones you would sieve the soil mixture. The filter is changed to take out the solid particles that have not passed through the filter.

KEY FACTS

You can use a sieve to sort solid particles of different sizes. This is what Kelly's mum is doing.

You can also use the filter to separate solids from air. This is what Bill's dad is doing. Filtering is a way of separating very fine solid particles from liquid from air.

★ Tip 1

To separate oil and water, just let the oil float on top of the water. Pour off the oil from the top.

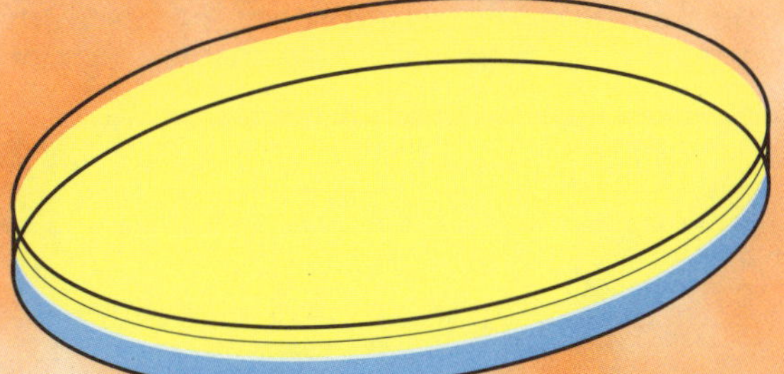

★ Tip 2

Solutions will pass through filter paper. So salty water will not be affected by going through a filter.

In a solution the solid particles are small enough to go through the paper.

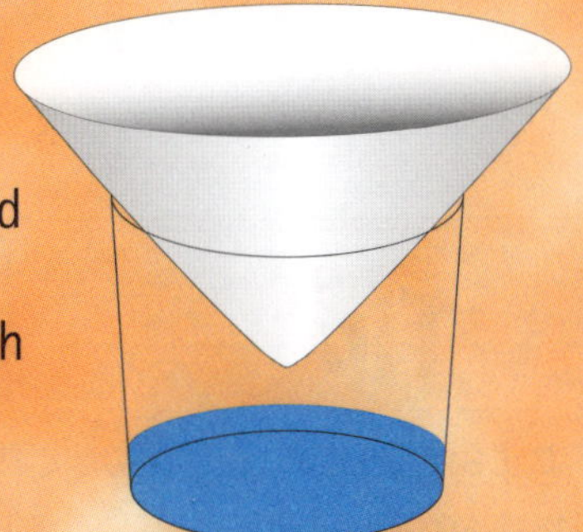

Air resistance

Achieved?

At Level 4 you should be able to say how the force of air resistance slows moving objects.

Let's practise!

Question:

a) Bob drops two sheets of paper. One is dropped flat. The other is scrunched into a ball. He drops them at the same time from the same height. Which one do you think will hit the ground first? Explain your idea.

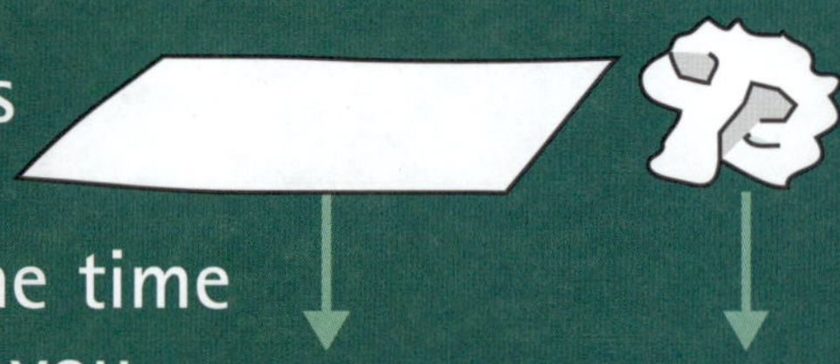

b) Meena uses scrap writing paper to make balls. She makes one ball small and tight. She makes one large and loose. She throws the balls. Which ball do you think she will be able to throw furthest? Explain your idea.

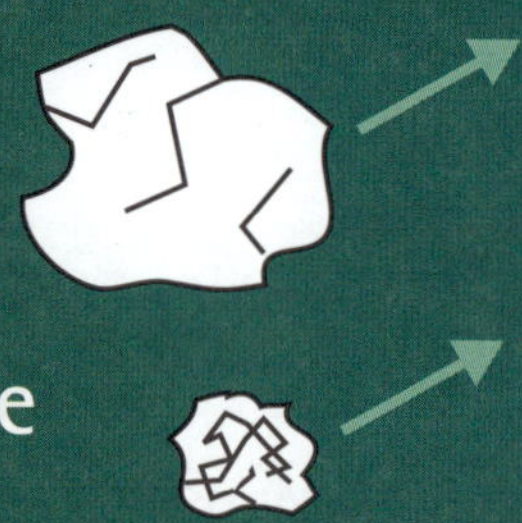

1. Read the question then read it again.

   These questions are connected because they are about the **same force**.

2. Picture the question. What does it tell you?

   In both cases one of the objects is **larger**, and so has **more air resistance**, than the other.

3. Remember the key facts.

   Air resistance **slows** objects that fall or move through the air. The **bigger** the object, the more it is **affected** by air resistance.

4. Work through the problem.

   The flat sheet will have much more air resistance than the screwed up ball. This will mean that it is **affected** more by air resistance. It will fall more slowly. When Meena throws the balls, the large loose one will be affected more by air resistance.

★ Tip

Big parachutes slow objects better than small ones.

Magnetic attraction and repulsion

Achieved?

At Level 4 you have to know about magnetic forces.
For example: that like poles repel and unlike poles attract.

Let's practise!

Question: Paula had two bar magnets. Each magnet had a blue end and a red end. Red = North and Blue = South.

- What happens if she moves the red and blue ends together?
- If she moves the two blue ends together?
- If she moves the two red ends together?

1. Read the question then read it again.

   The red end **attracts** the blue.

2. Picture the question. What does it tell you?

   There is a force pushing **like** ends apart.
   There is a force pulling **unlike** ends together.

3. Study magnetic poles.

   The red and blue ends are really called the **poles** of the magnet. The red pole is always the north pole of the magnet and the blue end is the south pole of the magnet.

4. Remember the key facts.

   Like poles repel and unlike poles attract.

5. Work through the problem.

   Unlike magnetic poles attract. Like magnetic poles repel.

★ Tip

Always use the correct words about magnets:

Poles are the ends of the magnet.

Attract is the correct word. Do not say 'stick'.

Repel is the correct word for 'push apart'.

Magnetic sorting

Achieved?

At Level 4 you have to know which metals are magnetic and which are not.

Let's practise!

Question: Ravi tests materials to see which are attracted to a magnet. He sorts them into two sets. All of the set that are attracted to magnets are metal. He lists the different metals.

Metal – used for	Does it conduct electricity?	Is it attracted to magnets?
aluminium – foil	✓	✗
steel – scissors	✓	✓
copper – pipes	✓	✗
silver – rings	✓	✗
iron – nails	✓	✓

List the metals that are magnetic and list the metals that are not magnetic.

1. Read the question then read it again.
2. Picture the question. What does it tell you?
3. Study metals.
4. Remember the key facts.
5. Work through the problem.

No non-metals are magnetic. Some metals are attracted to magnets.

All you have to do is write two lists.

Find out as much as you can about types of metals and what they are used for.

Iron and steel are the only magnetic metals.

Metals attracted to magnets	Metals not attracted to magnets
iron	copper
steel	silver
	aluminium

★ Tip

When testing metals, if one is attracted to a magnet it must have iron or steel in it. Tin cans only have a very thin layer of tin over an inside of steel.

Making electrical circuits

Achieved?

At Level 4 you need to describe and explain the way electrical devices, such as bulbs and batteries, are connected in a circuit.

Let's practise!

Question: Jim connected a bulb into four circuits. Tick the box next to the circuits that will work. Put a cross in the box next to the circuits that will not work.

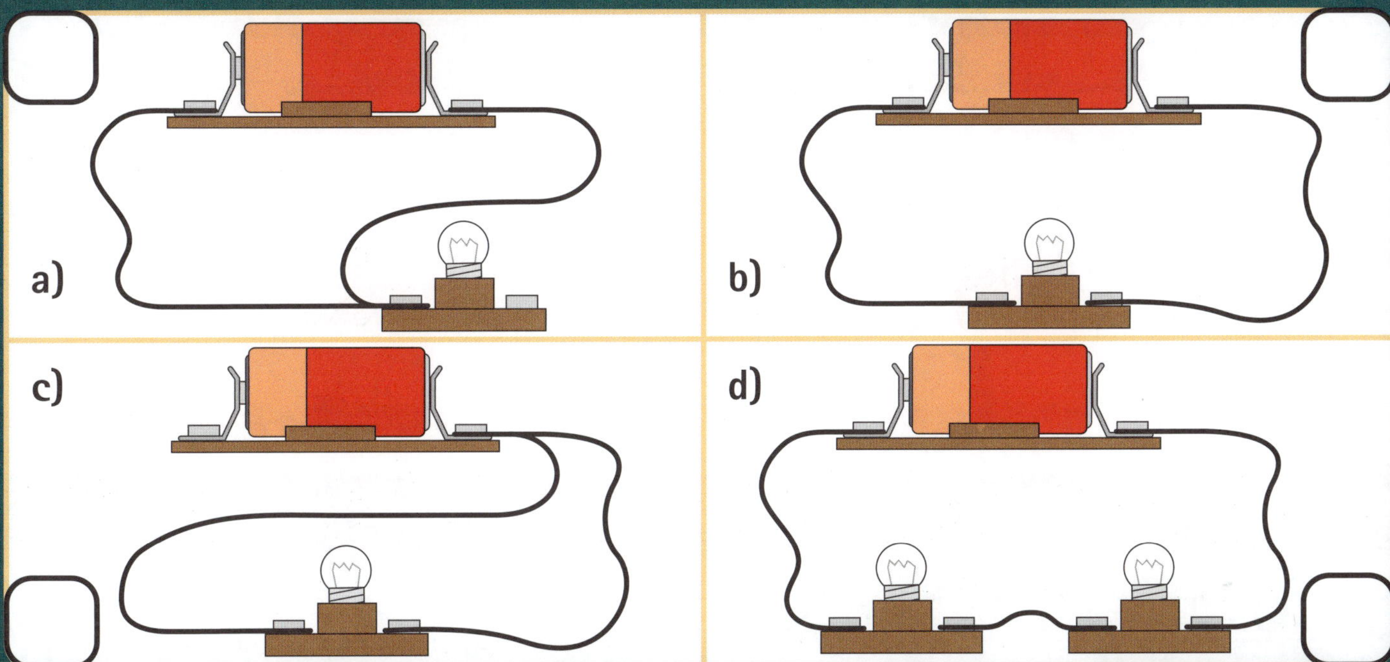

Explain why you have ticked or crossed each circuit.

1. Read the question then read it again.
2. Remember the key facts.
3. Work through the problem.

Look at the drawings of circuits. Two of these circuits will work but the other two will not.

For **the electrical current** to **flow**, it must go in one **terminal** of a bulb or battery and out of the other terminal.

Follow the path for the electricity all round the circuit. If there is not a **complete pathway**, then the electricity will not flow and the bulb will not glow.

Electrical switches

Achieved?

At Level 4 you need to describe and explain the way electrical devices, such as switches, are connected in a circuit.

Let's practise!

Question: Karen connected a switch into three circuits.
Tick the box next to the circuits where the bulb is glowing. Put a cross in the box next to the circuits where the bulb is not glowing.

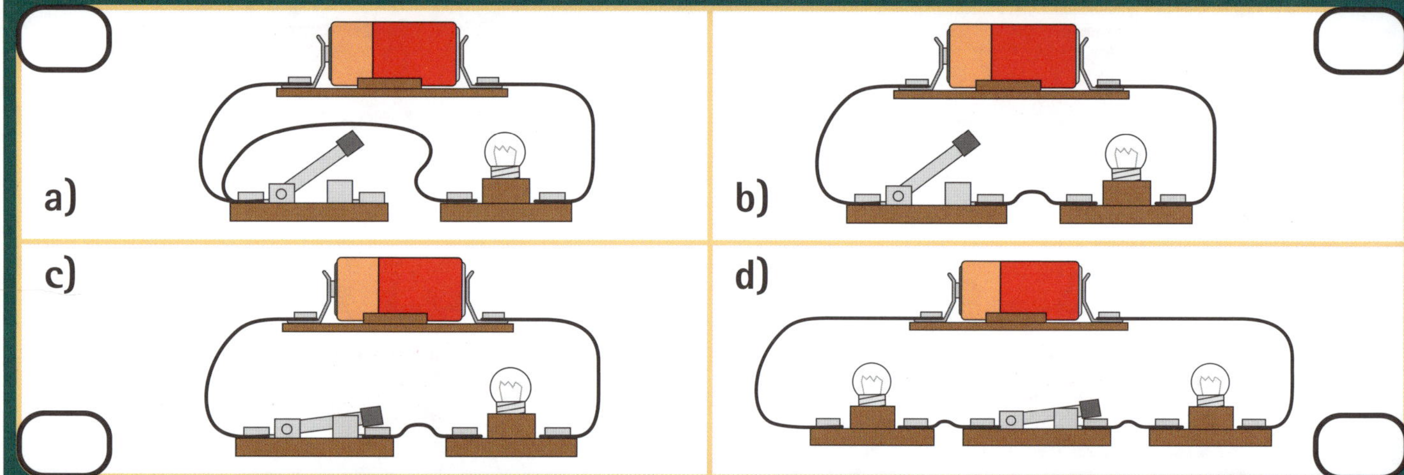

Explain why you have ticked or crossed each circuit.

1. Read the question then read it again.
2. Remember the key facts.
3. Work through the problem.

The most important part of the drawings is the switch. Look carefully at the way it is connected.

For **electricity** to **flow**, it must go in one **terminal** of a bulb or battery and out of the other terminal.

Concentrate on the switch. If the switch is open then electricity cannot pass through. Follow the path for the electricity all round the circuit. If there is not a complete pathway, then the electrical current will not flow and the bulb will not glow.

Tip

In circuit a, the switch is not part of the circuit so the bulb lights.

The position of the Sun

Achieved?

At Level 4 you should be able to describe the way the Sun appears to move.

Let's practise!

Question: These two drawings show the shadow of a stick at different times on a sunny day.
Match the time of day to the shadow.
Why do shadows change during the day?
Tick one box.

- ☐ The Sun moves.
- ☐ The Sun rises and sets.
- ☐ The Earth turns on its axis.

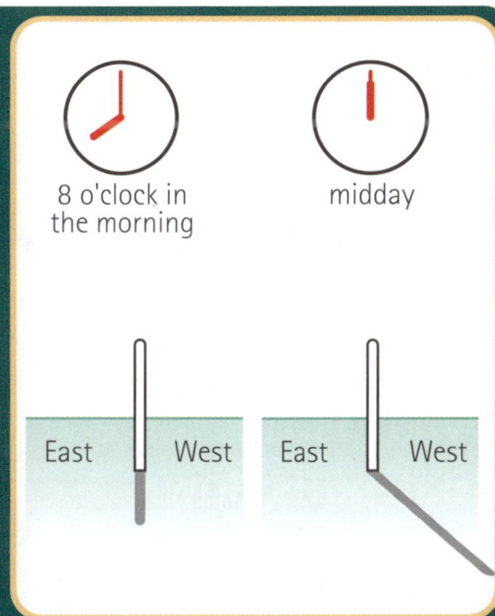

1. Read the question then read it again.
   There are two parts. Draw the line first. Now think about explaining why shadows change.
2. Picture the question. What does it tell you?
   Stand a pole in your playground or in a place you know near your home. Do the shadows change position during a sunny day?
3. Remember the key facts.
   The **Earth rotates** on its **axis**. This causes day and night. We say the Sun rises in the east and sets in the west. In the mornings and evenings the Sun is low in the sky and the shadows are long. At midday (noon) the Sun is high in the sky and the shadows are short.
4. Work through the problem.
   Decide which drawing is noon (short shadow). The other must be morning. Now say why shadows change. This is to do with the rotation of the Earth making it seem as if the Sun moves.

★ Tip

Remember to think about looking SOUTH when talking about the Sun's movement. East is then to your left and west is to your right. You can tell which way south is because the Sun will be shining from that direction at lunchtime. Use your ruler to line up the light source with the object blocking it. Draw the shadow after the object.

Weighing

Achieved?

At Level 4 you should be able to describe the effects of the pull of gravity.

Let's practise!

Question: Ann is weighing objects with a spring balance. She records the weight of each object in a chart.

Which object weighs the most?

What units do we use for weight?

What is the force that pulls down on the objects?

Object	Weight (newtons)
drinks bottle	6
scissors	0.5
boots	4
tub of clay	13

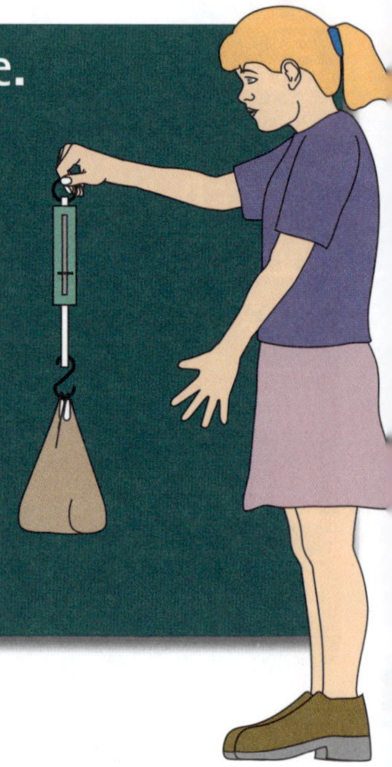

1. Read the question then read it again.
   - Most of the information you need is in the table.
2. Picture the question. What does it tell you?
   - Think about which of these objects is heaviest. Which object stretched the string most?
3. Work through the problem.
   - Look carefully at the table. The units of weight are shown at the top of the second column (newtons).
4. Remember the key facts.
   - The pull of the Earth's gravity on objects is measured as their weight. When you step on a balance that shows your weight, you are squashing a spring. If you are heavy you will squash the spring a lot. If you are light the spring will be squashed less.

Tip

The pull of gravity depends on where you are. If you are on the Moon there is less gravity and you weigh less. If you could stand on Jupiter you would weigh more because there is a much stronger pull of gravity.

KEY FACTS

Gravity pulls objects. An object can either squash or stretch a spring.

Friction

Achieved?

To achieve Level 4 you have to know that forces stop objects moving. For example: friction stops a book, which is on a slope, from sliding.

Let's practise!

Question: Look at this drawing. The toy car is not moving. Jim thinks that the toy just won't move. Rashid thinks the toy won't move because of air resistance acting against it. Sara thinks it will not move because of friction.
Who do you think is correct?
Why do you think this?

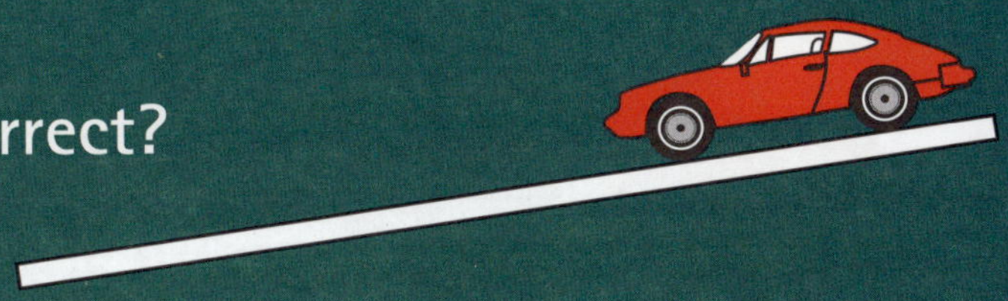

1. Read the question then read it again.
2. Picture the question. What does it tell you?
3. Think of an everyday example.

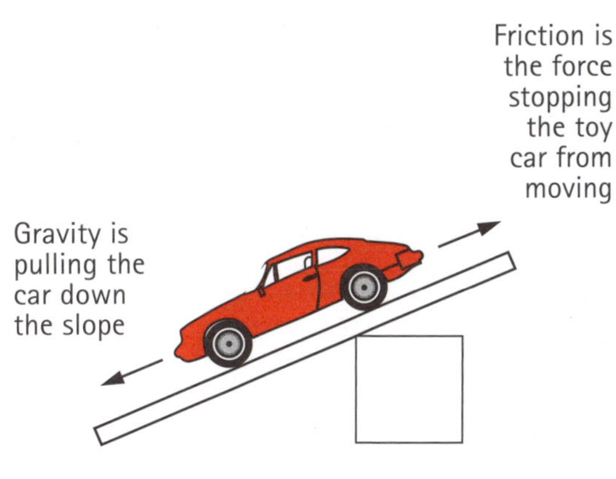

Put a toy on a tray. It will only move when one end of the tray is lifted.

KEY FACTS

friction – a force which tries to stop things moving against or through each other

surface friction – when a solid tries to slide against another solid

air resistance – when a solid tries to slide through a gas, e.g. air

water resistance – when a solid tries to move through a liquid (e.g. water)

Tip

Gravity works all the time on all objects. Things will fall unless a force stops them. **Air resistance** slows the fall of an object that falls through the air.

Friction force

Achieved?

At Level 4 you should be able to say how moving things are affected by forces like friction.

Let's practise!

Question: Kate made a slide out of cotton for her toy. She attached the toy to the slide with a paperclip. She let it slide down the cotton runway.

a) What force pulled the toy down the slide?

b) She made a second slide out of rough string. What do you think will happen to the toy? Explain your idea.

1. Read the question then read it again.
   There are several parts to the question. Make sure you answer each part.
2. Picture the question. What does it tell you?
   The slide was made of smooth cotton and it was sloping downwards.
3. Remember the key facts.
   Gravity pulls objects towards the Earth. The fact that they go down a slope does not change this. Whenever an object moves, it is slowed by friction. This is caused by rubbing between two surfaces. The cotton is smooth so there is not much friction.
4. Work through the problem.
   The rough string will have more friction. Carefully slide some cotton between your finger. Now do the same with rough string. Which causes most rubbing?

★ Tip

Very thin, slippery nylon fishing line makes great slides. Take care though to put it where no one will walk into it.

KEY FACTS

When rough objects rub, there is more friction.

The size of shadows

Achieved?

At Level 4 you should be able to describe the way shadows change.

Let's practise!

Question: The clown is in the crew's spotlight.

The only light comes from a single spot.

What happens to the length of the clown's shadow as he walks away from the light?

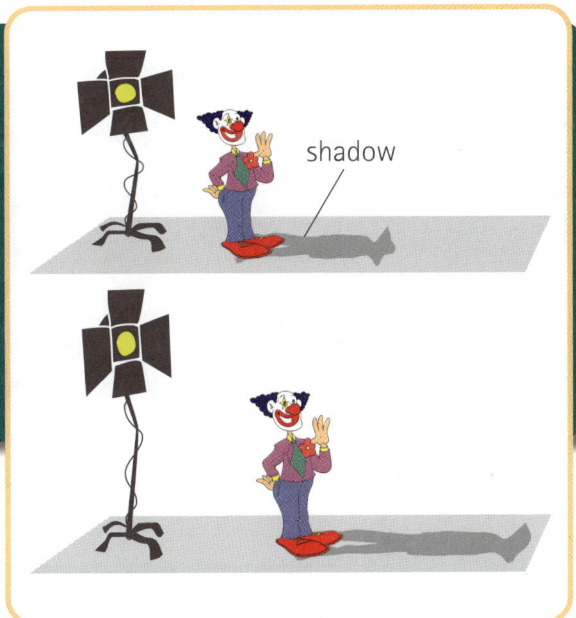

1. Read the question then read it again.
2. Picture the question. What does it tell you?
3. Remember the key facts.
4. Think of other examples.

Concentrate on the length of his shadow as he is further away. Compare it with the **shadow** he makes in the first drawing.

Draw a line to show how much **light** he will be **blocking out** in each case.

Shadows are formed when light is blocked. You make **sharp** shadows where there is **one strong light source**.

Link this with page 49, which asks about what happens when the light source moves.

KEY FACTS

Shadows are formed when light is **blocked**.

When a light source is directly overhead we see no shadow. Shadows are longest when the light is at a shallow angle.

★ Tip

Practise making shadows with a small toy and a torch. How many ways can you find to make the shadow bigger and smaller?

Opaque and transparent

Achieved?

At Level 4 you need to know that light will pass through transparent materials and not through those which are opaque.

Let's practise!

Question: Leo and Ravi hold a book and an empty clear bottle in front of light.

The book makes a dark shadow.

The bottle makes a faint shadow.

Explain why one of the shadows is dark and the other is faint.

In the boxes below write T if the object is transparent and O if the object is opaque.

- ☐ glass of water
- ☐ brick wall
- ☐ glass of milk
- ☐ window blind
- ☐ mirror

1. Read the question then read it again.
2. Picture the question. What does it tell you?
3. Remember the key facts.
4. Work through the problem.

Think about the way in which light will **pass through** some materials but not others.

Light is being **blocked** by one of the objects in the first part of the question. Light is passing through the other object.

Transparent means that light will pass through it. **Opaque** means that light will be blocked.

Which materials are transparent and which are opaque? Transparent materials do not make much of a **shadow**.

Tip

Don't think that all solid things are opaque. The two words have very different meanings. Glass is one example of a transparent solid.

Sounds through different materials

Achieved?

At Level 4 you should be able to say how sound travels through different materials.

Let's practise!

Question:

a) Leo asks Kate to scratch the table gently. He can hardly hear her. What is the sound travelling **through** to reach his ear?

b) He puts his ear to the table. He can hear much better now. Explain this.

c) He puts a scarf between his ear and the table. He cannot hear the scratching at all now. Explain why the sound is not reaching his ear.

1. Picture the question. What does it tell you?

   Leo can only just hear the sound through the air (which is a gas). He can hear it better through the table (which is a solid).

2. Remember the key facts.

   Sound has to travel through something.
   It can travel through:

   gases – we know this because air is a mixture of gases

   solids – when we use string telephones the sound travels down the solid string

   liquids – whales and dolphins communicate underwater using sound

3. Work through the problem.

   The scarf is a solid but it is very soft and fluffy. Sounds travel well through hard solids like the table – soft materials absorb sound and do not transmit it well.

★ Tip

Think about the old cowboy films. Trackers would put their ear to the ground to try to detect the sound of horses' hooves as sound which travels better through rock than through the air.

Sounds we hear

Achieved?

At Level 4 you should be able to say how sound travels to our ears.

Let's practise!

Question:

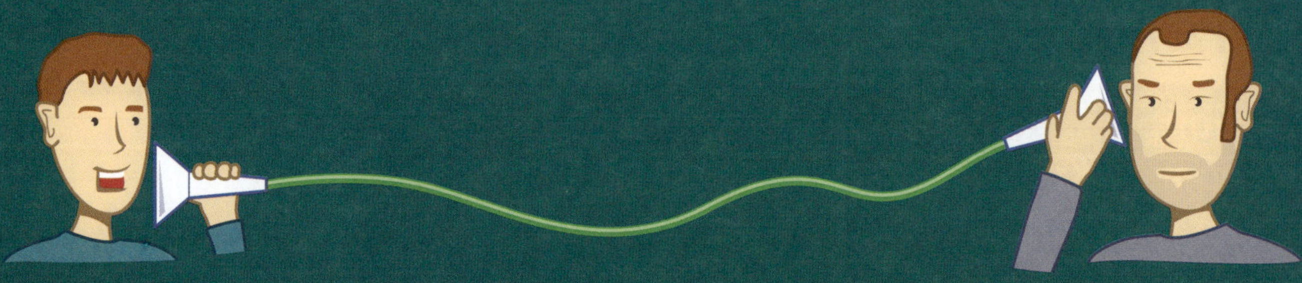

Paul and his dad have emptied all the water from a hose. They have put funnels on each end. They say they can hear each other really well through the hose. Use the diagram to help you explain how this works.

1. Picture the question.

Sound **spreads out**. Think of the sound trapped in the hose and not able to spread out – it can only escape when it reaches the other end.

2. Remember the key facts.

Sound travels through **air** to reach our ears. It gets **fainter** as you move further away from the sound because it **spreads out**. Anything that stops it spreading out will help us to hear.

3. Think of other examples.

In the old days, before phones were used, the ship's captain spoke to the engine room down a speaking tube. This is just the same idea as the hose and funnels!

Tip

Make a big funnel out of paper and see if this helps you to hear someone whispering across the room.
Spies might use ideas like this to overhear secrets.

Sounds are caused by vibrations

Achieved?

At Level 4 you should be able to describe how all sounds are made when an object vibrates.

Let's practise!

Question:
Explain how percussion instruments work.

Jim taps a triangle. It vibrates and makes a sound.
How can Jim stop it vibrating?

Put a few grains of rice on a biscuit tin lid.
Tap it gently. Explain what happens.

1. Read the question then read it again.

   This question and activity are about vibrations.

2. Picture the question. What does it tell you?

   Vibrating objects produce sounds. By holding an object firmly you stop it vibrating.

3. Remember the key facts.

   It is hard to see an object vibrating, but you can feel it if you touch it gently.

4. Think of another example.

   When you twang a ruler you can see it wobble back and forwards. This is vibration. In the ruler it is slow enough to see.

Tip

Put some grains of salt on the sealed end of a safe empty tin. See what happens when you make a loud noise near the tin or touch the tin with a vibrating tuning fork.

KEY FACTS

Percussion instruments are those which vibrate after being tapped.

KEY FACTS Sc1

At Level 3 you need to be able to:

- put forward your own ideas to answer a question
- know why it is important to gather data to answer questions
- make observations
- use simple measuring equipment
- carry out a fair test with help
- record observations in a variety of ways
- explain observations
- suggest improvements to your work

At Level 4 you need to be able to:

- see that you need evidence to support scientific ideas
- decide on the best way to do an experiment or test
- make good predictions
- select the most important information
- choose the best equipment for a test
- record observations and measurements
- draw and make sense of a bar chart
- come to conclusions
- say ways in which work can be improved

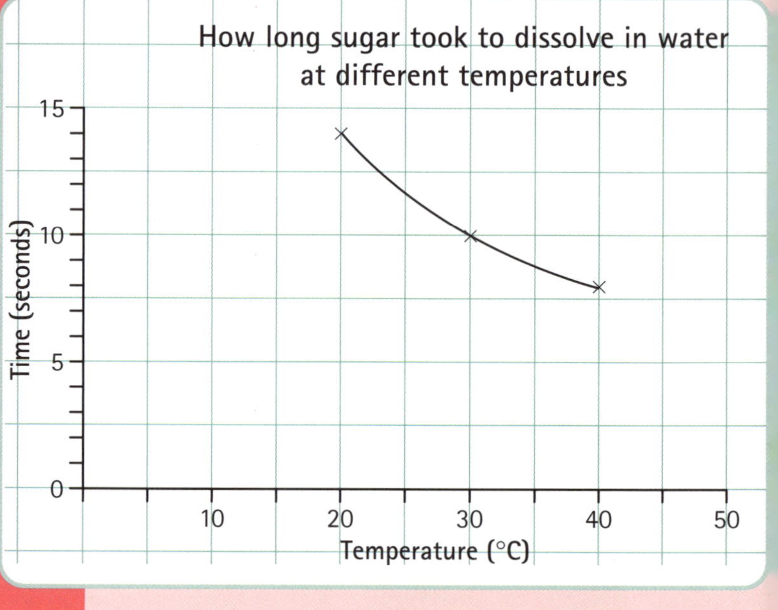

KEY FACTS Sc2

At Level 3 you need to know:

- about basic life processes
- the differences between living and non-living things
- reasons for changes in living things, such as diet and water supply
- the ways in which animals are suited to their environment

At Level 4 you need to know:

- the names of some of the organs of the human body
- the position of some of the organs of the human body
- the names and position of some of the organs of a variety of plants
- how to use simple keys to identify living things
- how to put living things into groups
- about food chains

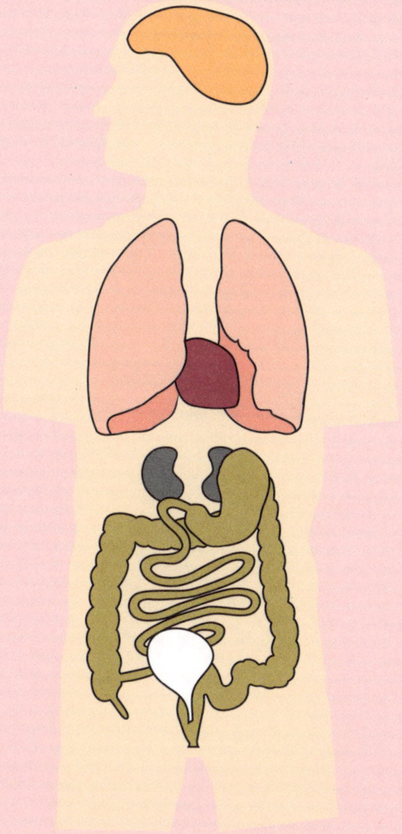

KEY FACTS Sc3

At Level 3 you need to know:

- how to put forward your own ideas to answer a question
- about sorting materials into groups
- why some materials are suited to a particular purpose
- which changes can be reversed
- which changes cannot be reversed

At Level 4 you need to know:

- that you need evidence to support scientific ideas
- about the properties of materials
- how materials are classified into solids, liquids and gases
- how to separate simple mixtures
- the scientific words used to describe changes, such as condense, evaporate and freeze
- which changes are easily reversed and which changes are difficult to reverse

KEY FACTS Sc4

At Level 3 you need to know:

- the causes and effects in physical processes, such as a bulb not lighting because of a break in the circuit
- about forces changing the direction or speed of movement
- the effects of sound and light, such as the way they get fainter as the sources become more distant

At Level 4 you need to know:

- how to alter electrical circuits
- how the Sun changes position during the day
- that objects are attracted by gravity
- which things are attracted by magnets
- that magnets can attract and repel each other
- how shadows are formed
- that sounds travel through a variety of materials

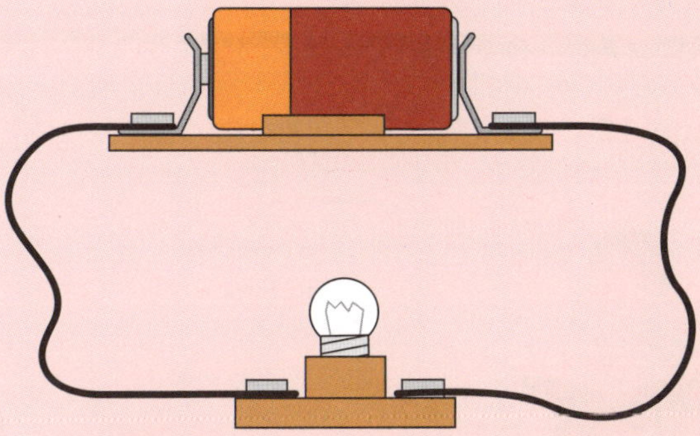

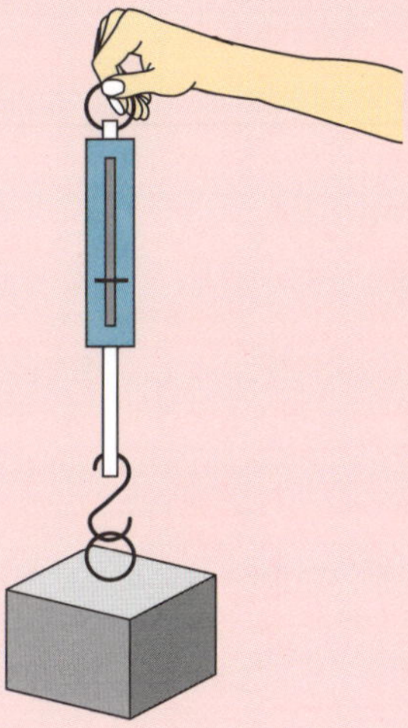

Answers

Page 12

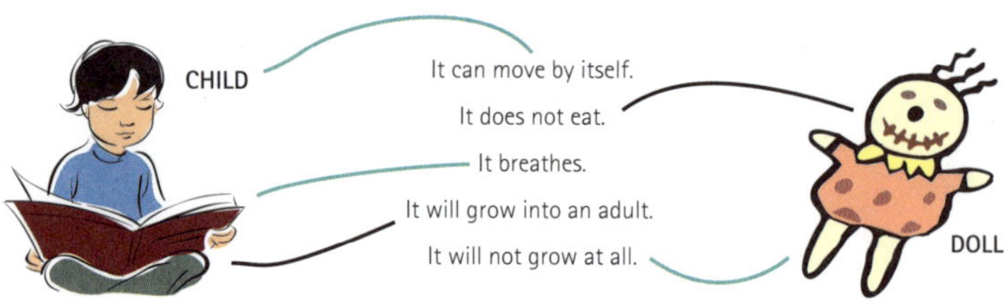

Page 18

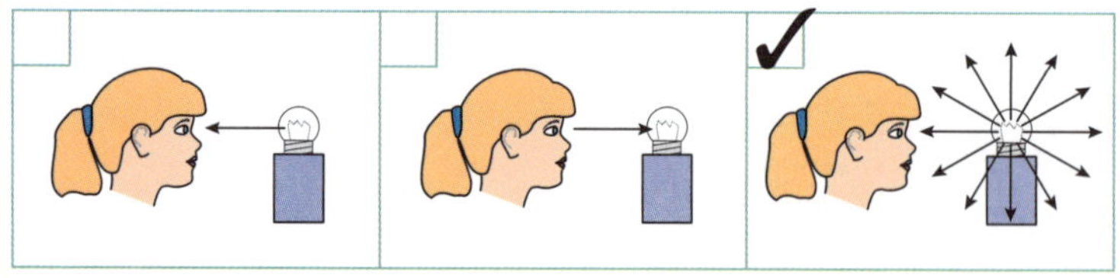

Page 22

a) ✓ : The width of the paper strip and the length of the paper strip.

b) ✓ 1 gram masses and 10 gram masses.

Page 14

a)

brass steel	wood plastic
conducts electricity	does not conduct electricity

b)

Page 23

a) Do large parachutes fall more slowly than small ones?

b) The table shows that the larger the area of the parachute, the longer it takes to fall so larger parachutes do fall more slowly than smaller ones.

Page 24

a) 10 seconds

b) 8 seconds

c) The graph shows that the hotter the water, the faster the sugar dissolves.

Page 15

Material	What it is like	What it can be used for
perspex	soft and warm	bike tyres
copper	heavy and strong	windows
rubber	see-through	clothes
cotton	conducts electricity	garden walls
stone	bouncy and hard wearing	electrical wires

Page 25

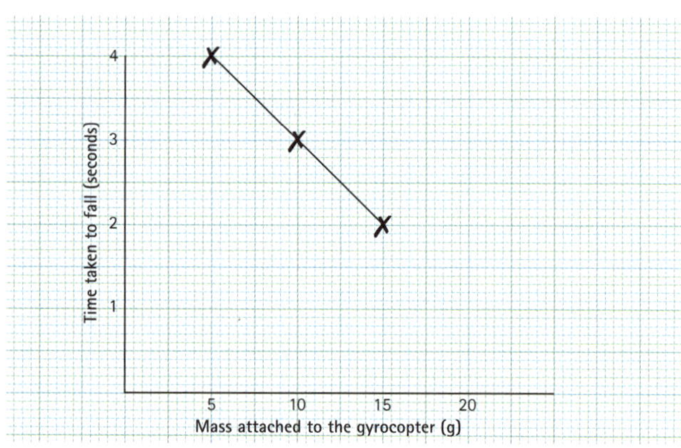

Page 16

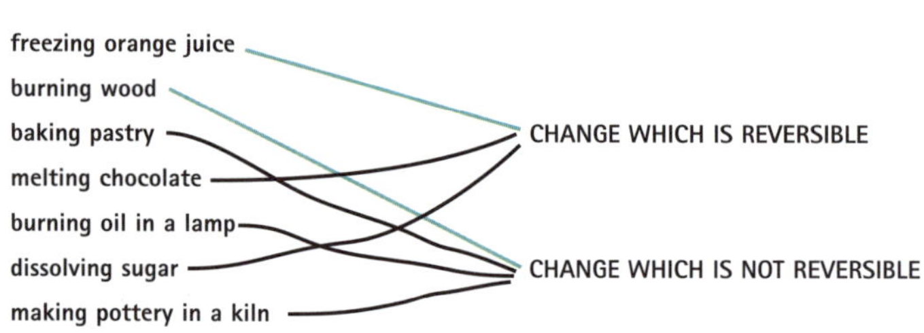

Page 27

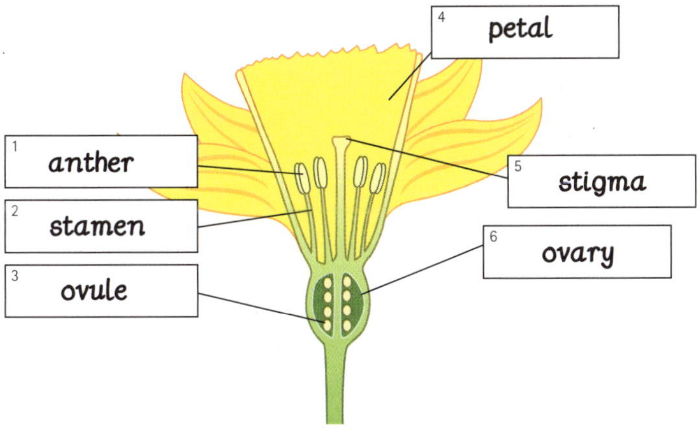

Page 28

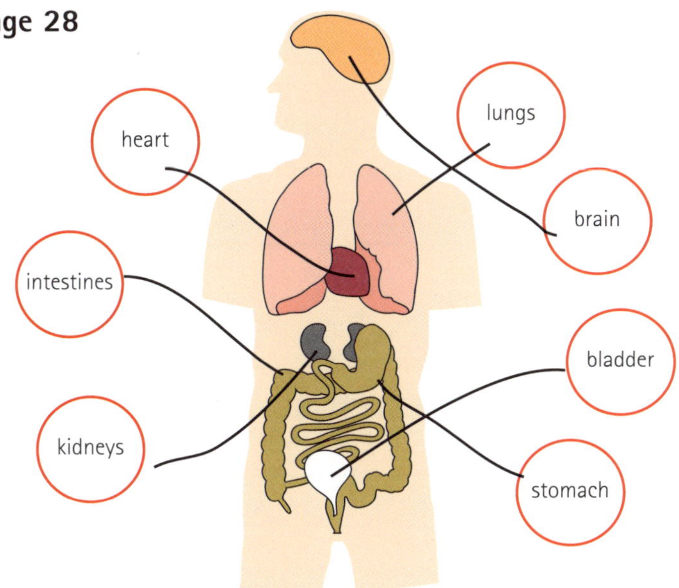

Page 30

mammal (hairy with four legs)
dog lion

bird (feathers with two legs)
eagle vulture

reptile (scaly skin)
tortoise crocodile

insect (six legs)
bee butterfly

Page 31

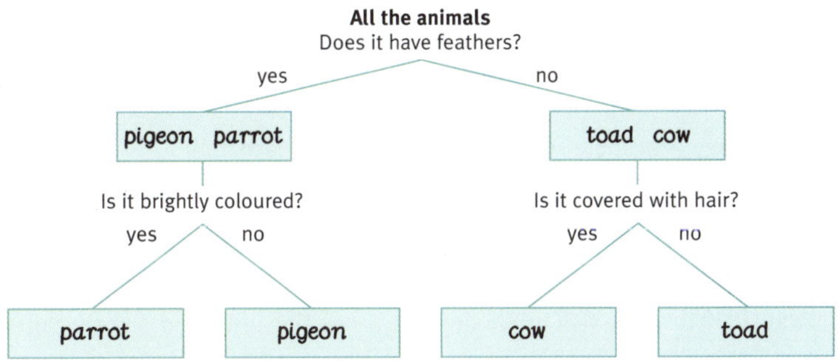

Page 32

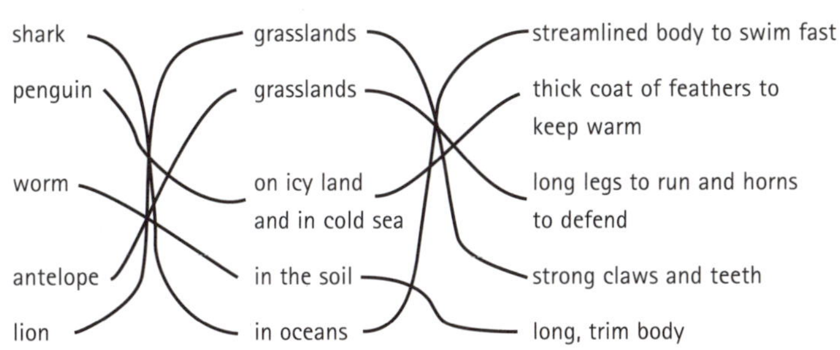

Page 33

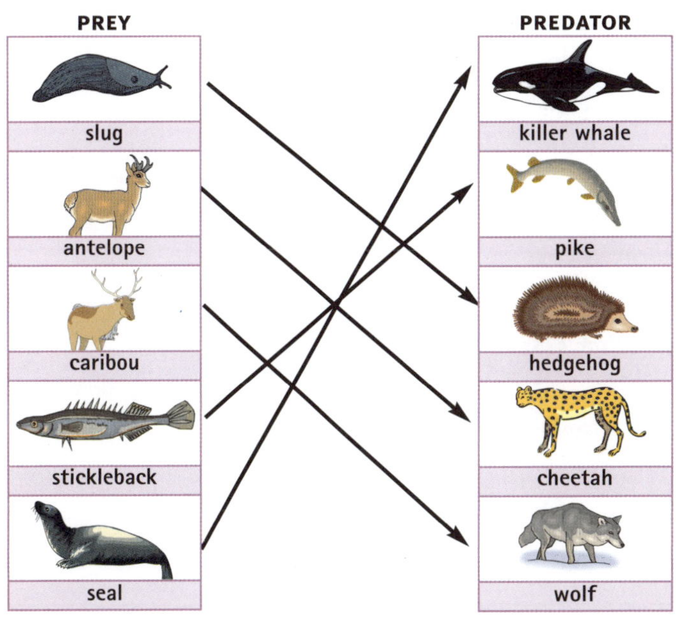

Page 34

Sun ➜ wheat ➜ chicken ➜ human

Sun ➜ grass ➜ cow ➜ human

e.g. Sun ➜ orange tree ➜ orange juice ➜ human

Page 35

The turkey is in the **bird** group because it **has feathers.**

The beetle is in the **insect** group because it **has six legs.**

The mole is in the **mammal** group because it **has hair and feeds its young on milk.**

The shark is in the **fish** group because it **has fins, gills and a scaly tail.**

The snake is in the **reptile** group because it **has a scaly body.**

The rabbit is in the **mammal** group because it **has hair and feeds its young on milk**

Page 38

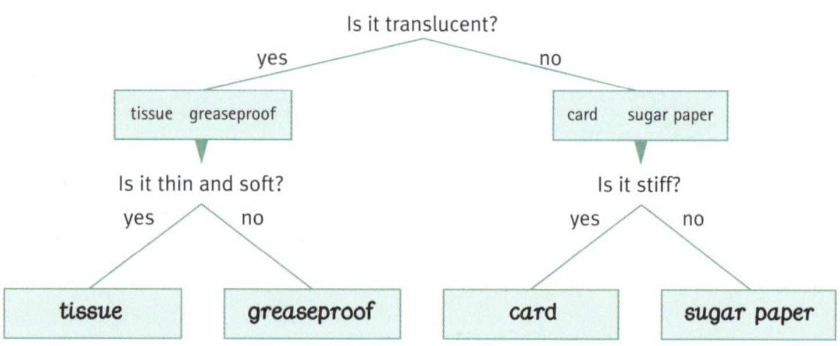

Page 40

a) Tick 'salt' and 'instant tea'

b) Tick 'Stir the mixture' and 'Use hot water'.

Page 41

Solid at room temperature	Liquid at room temperature	Gas at room temperature
volcanic lava	oil	oxygen
ice cream	milk	helium
stone	shampoo	hydrogen
paper		
chocolate		

Page 47

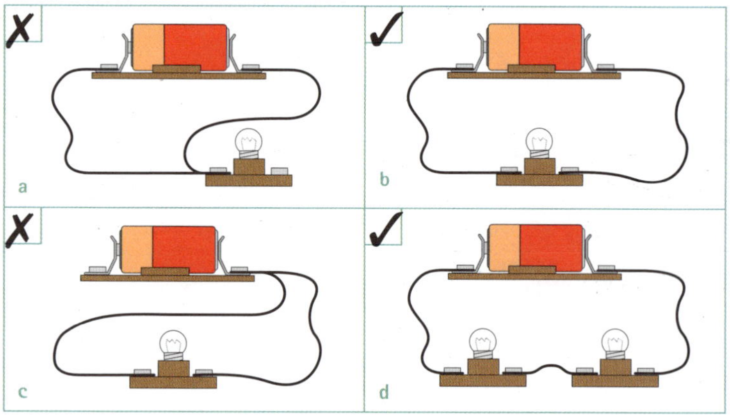

Page 48

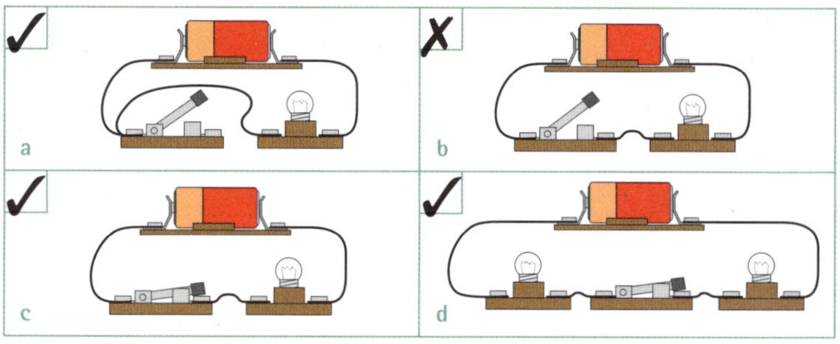

Page 54

a) The shadow made by the bottle is light because some light is getting through the transparent bottle.

b) Glass of water is transparent, the rest are opaque.